Buried

by the

Church

Neal Sutton

The astonishing secrets behind the building and
the builders of the Pyramids
The real lives of Jesus Christ; his wife, Mary Magdalene
and the Egyptian High Priest John 'the Baptist'
The rise and lies of the Church of Rome
The role of the Knights Templar and the
Ark of the Covenant
Troubled times to come for a planet in spiritual turmoil
And the truth about your spirituality that
the Church of Rome
does not want you to know

Matador
9 Priory Business Park,
Wistow Road, Kibworth Beauchamp,
Leicestershire. LE8 0RX
Tel: (+44) 116 279 2299
Fax: (+44) 116 279 2277
Email: books@troubador.co.uk
Web: www.troubador.co.uk/matador

ISBN 978 1780882 338

British Library Cataloguing in Publication Data.
A catalogue record for this book is available from the British Library.

Typeset in 11pt Adobe Garamond Pro by Troubador Publishing Ltd, Leicester, UK

Matador is an imprint of Troubador Publishing Ltd

Printed and bound in the UK by TJ International, Padstow, Cornwall

To my grandmother,

Marjorie Curry,

My inspiration and my guiding light,

And to my family, with love.

Contents

Introduction

Thank you for taking the time and trouble to read my little book. I have written this book for everyone, for I believe that everyone should read it. I am especially keen for agnostics and atheists to give it a try, for I am certain that they too will experience the fundamental truth that is contained within it.

Atheists and agnostics do not believe in God or life after death – or at least they have reservations about it all. The idea of God and life after death that they do not believe in is the one promoted by the Church, for amazingly it is the only interpretation and the only source with which anyone has the opportunity to believe in a higher power or some kind of greater force at work. It therefore, incredibly, is the only concept most people consider when making their decision on whether or not they believe in 'God'.

This 'one horse' concept is spoon-fed to us all from birth. It is the culture into which we are born. From the time that we are babies and our families talk about religion, the only concept of God and life after death that is actively promoted is that of the religious institutions. Every village and town has a church or many churches. All of them promote the same idea of life after death and 'God': Be good and accept Jesus as your saviour, and you will be 'saved'. Saved from an eternity in hell, to reside in heaven forever. A heaven with God on his throne and Jesus at his side, the Devil residing in hell far below, alongside everyone who was bad in their lives. This is life after death – believe in this or believe in nothing at all.

The church offers no proof of this concept. They cannot tell you for certain, despite the fact that one claims direct authority from Jesus Christ, himself purportedly the son of God.

Churches are treading a dangerous path. Their obsession with subservience through guilt and the active promotion of myth is harmful to everyone. The atheists and agnostics are not entirely wrong not to believe in a God based on these stories, some of which stretch the human capability of belief, based upon blind faith, to the limits and beyond!

The agnostic or the atheist does not believe in this 2,000-year-old, nationwide, almost worldwide, promotion of the idea of a vengeful God and a life in heaven or hell, based upon one shot at redemption. For the agnostic and the atheist are 'rational thinkers', and when faced with the fables and the miracles the sheer implausibility of it all, the monumental leap of faith required by such a belief system, leaves them with no alternative but to remain atheist.

But what if the truth about life after death and this vengeful God was somewhat different? If the myth was stripped away, if the half-truths and downright lies told by the Church were exposed and a concept of life after death that fitted the universal order was revealed, how many then would be atheist or agnostic?

Enjoy.

Neal Sutton

The journey begins

On any given Sunday people all over the country, and indeed the world, make their way to church. Village churches, city cathedrals, Roman Catholic churches, Jewish synagogues, Seven Day Adventists, Baptists, Methodists. For most, Sunday is the day to worship God and Jesus, and of course some will also attend church on other days.

Jesus born of a virgin, performed miracles, raised Lazarus from the dead, then was persecuted and crucified, they will tell you, for *your* sins. Christians and a myriad of cults from the Plymouth Brethren to the Jehovah's Witnesses all put their stamp on what the Bible actually means. They have all interpreted its contents their way and attempt to exert control over our lives according to their particular interpretation. They promise us an eternity in a lake of fire if we disobey their various rules.

There are over 300 religions in full swing on this planet at this time and their rules and commandments vary wildly. Which one, if any, is correct, definitely and beyond refute? *Definite* is a powerful word because it removes totally the need for faith, and faith is what all religions are built on. It is their first demand: You must have faith. Therefore, by the very interpretation, *definite* you cannot be.

When I first started to ask questions of religion and its origins, the first thing I was told was that I should have faith. I should have faith in the Gospels and faith in the whole of the Bible, 'for that is the word of God himself'. Faith, it appeared, was all I needed. Indeed it was absolutely necessary to have faith, for some of the stories and events portrayed in the Bible defy any kind of logic. Faith alone: Just believe in it all, blindly, and off to heaven you will go.

But was I really to believe in a virgin birth? That God himself had 'planted the seed inside her'? Was I really to believe in the story of the Garden of Eden? Was I really to believe that Christ was the son of God and was crucified for our sins and that this was his sole purpose in coming to Earth? What was God thinking of? Couldn't he find a better way to enlighten us, because he really should have known that it wouldn't work!

Contradictions

The more I studied the Bible and asked questions of the faithful, the more hostile was their response. I asked, if the Bible is the word of God and we are to *add not one word nor take one word away*, why are there so many contradictions within? The main four gospels in the New Testament differ immensely on the birth of Jesus and the crucifixion. They all have a different slant on the 'resurrection'. Some Biblicists contend that biblical chronology fixes the date of creation at 4004BC, thereby making the Earth about 6,000 years old. Some present-day Creationists stubbornly adhere to a young Earth timetable in spite of overwhelming evidence that the Earth is actually many millions of years old.

Creation stories/myths abound in cultures throughout the world. In Australia, the Aboriginal myth consists of a huge serpent that comes out of the water and spews forth man and woman from his mouth.

Let us study more closely the story of Adam and Eve. Immediately noticeable is that it is here, at the very start of the Bible, that things start to go wrong for the female in the Christian Church. No matter how incredulous the whole thing about Eve being created from Adam's rib, churchgoers the world over stubbornly believe in the Bible's version of events.

First let's take a closer look at the story as laid down in the Bible. God said to Adam:

> 'From every tree you may eat but the tree in the midst of Paradise do not eat, for the day that you eat from it you will surely die.' But the serpent was wiser than all the animals that were in Paradise, and he persuaded Eve, saying, 'On the day when you eat from the tree which is in the midst of Paradise, the eyes of your mind will be opened.' And Eve obeyed... she ate; she also gave to her husband.

The next thing to happen is that God flies into a rage and curses the serpent, Eve, and Adam for what they have done. Nothing about this story stacks up. It just does not make any kind of sense when you take into account the qualities that the Bible and the Church bestows on 'God':

God is supposed to be Omniscient = having the capability of knowing everything infinitely, including thoughts, feelings, actions etc.

God is supposed to be Omnipotent = having unlimited power, and

God is supposed to be Omnipresent = having the ability to be in every place at every time.

That's a pretty tall order indeed but if he did possess those abilities and qualities then the story as written above just could not have taken place. From the time he told them not to partake of the fruit of that tree he should have known that they would. When he found out that they had he would not have been surprised or become angry because he would know already! But clearly, according to the Bible he had no prior knowledge of their actions until he confronted them.

Add to this the fact that the text clearly states that the serpent was the '*wisest*' of all the creatures, not the craftiest or the most devious or the most evil, but the wisest.

Plus it must be remembered that prior to eating the fruit Adam and Eve would have had no knowledge of right and wrong, so they should have been the last ones to be blamed.

This God does not appear to be an all-loving God, more of a jealous God, angry, and vengeful. This version of the fable is catastrophically flawed. Yet remarkably few people find it necessary to question the contents of the story as told.

God created the garden, the tree, Adam, Eve and the Serpent, so the only 'being' ultimately responsible for everything that happened including the so-called 'fall from grace' was God.

So why blame Eve?

The answer, though, is simple. The whole story is a skewed version of earlier incarnations of the Garden of Eden myth and it has been included with the sole purpose of making the female the wrongdoer and the scapegoat of the Christian Church, forever enabling it to regard women in general with disdain and contempt.

Eve was merely one of the players in a series of events of which

God should have known the outcome. His omniscience – his capacity to know everything infinitely – puts the blame for events that took place squarely back with him.

The story does not take into account omniscience at all and shows God in a very poor light indeed, almost incapable of the love and forgiveness that the religion is supposedly based upon.

But this series of events is crucial for the Bible writers' resolute and single-minded defamation of the female. It is critical and central for the belief system that was to be promoted with unflinching vigor later on.

Let's look at an alternative scenario – an alternate version.

Many of the texts found in the codices at Nag Hammadi in 1948 describe Eve as the spiritual principle in humanity who raises Adam from his purely material state.

From Hypostasis of the Archons:

> And the spirit-endowed woman came to Adam and spoke to him saying, 'Arise Adam.' And when he saw her he said, 'It is you who have given me life; you shall be called "Mother of the Living" – For it is she who is my mother. It is she who is the Physician, and the Woman, and She Who Has Given Birth.' Then the Female Spiritual Principle came in the snake, the instructor, and it taught them saying, 'You shall not die; for it was out of jealousy that he said this to you. Rather, your eyes shall open, and you shall become like Gods, recognizing Evil and Good.' And the arrogant ruler cursed the woman, and the snake.

So we know that the creation story found in our Bible is certainly not new; other religions have used it, but *none* of them have done so to the detriment of the female.

It appears to this writer that changing the creation story to demean the female is a deliberate attempt to strengthen the position of an emerging patriarchal church.

The above outlines just one of the problems I have with the Old Testament part of the Bible. Another example is the entire Cain and Abel story, which is riddled with contradictions. Why was the mark placed on Cain if he was one of only three people on the planet? And if he went off to another land to take himself a wife, where did she come from? Who created her? The story contradicts itself from line to line and is just not credible at all.

If faith is a sole requirement of religion then your belief that this section of the Bible is true and the irrefutable word of God demands of the reader a leap of faith of monumental proportions. Such a leap of faith would be an irreversible lurch into crass stupidity.

The Old Testament is riddled with improbable and sometimes impossible stories punctuated with the actions of a vengeful and malevolent God. Far from being an all-loving God, he seems to be a rather nasty deity. I fail to see how anyone seeking spirituality could find much inspiration there.

Then, in the New Testament, there is the problem of the obvious contradictions between the four main gospels concerning the birth of Jesus, as well as the detail of the crucifixion and just who was at the tomb and who said and did what at the time of the resurrection. Some authors make much of these differences, quoting them as proof that the whole thing is just a story.

This is an entirely different scenario to that of Cain and Abel. What we must bear in mind is that the gospels were written some 40 years after the event, and one of them at least was written by someone who wasn't even there. We can forgive, then, lapses in memory and small differences in recollection that don't really affect the outcome greatly. But the creation myth is just that – a myth, borrowed and amended but nonetheless a myth, and the Cain and Abel story is a fable relating to it.

Bible coding and literal interpretation

As well as all this there is the issue of Bible coding. It creates a severe problem when translators, readers and followers of various Christian religions interpret the Bible quite literally. This fundamental mistake has created and perpetuated misleading and dangerous dogma. *The more the various churches interpret and follow the writings in the Bible literally, the further from the truth they actually are.* Bible coding is an incredible thing to have to inform Christians of because it flies in the face of 2,000 years of incorrect teachings.

Perhaps one of the biggest misinterpretations is one that has the entire Christian religion wrongly believing in a virgin birth. Now, just sit for a moment and think about this. A *virgin* birth. The truth is somewhat different. But a virgin birth in a religion was not a new thing, even 2,000 years ago, as we shall see later. Such, though, is the power of belief, and that people believe in the virgin birth amply demonstrates the power of religion to convince followers that something is a fact no matter how incredulous.

The 52 tractates originally short-listed for inclusion in the New Testament as Gospels were written in the ancient Coptic language of Egypt during early Christian times. The Coptic museum in Cairo ascertained that they were in fact copies of much older works originally composed in Greek. The books were coded in such a way that would make them beyond

Roman understanding. Remember, Rome was an aggressor and an unwelcome master in many lands. Its law was ruthlessly imposed, so it became inevitable that secrecy and disguised language was often utilised in communications between unwilling citizens.

Indeed, some of the texts were discovered to have very early origins, incorporating traditions from before AD50. They tend to portray an environment very different to that described in the Bible. The cities of Sodom and Gomorrah, for instance, are not presented as centres of wickedness and debauchery, but as cities of great wisdom and learning.

The following table lists words contained within the Bible that are commonly misinterpreted, drastically altering the religious perception of the events in which they are contained. The whole perception of not only the people involved but the also events that took place, why and how are seriously in error.

The Church has known of these misinterpretations since the time of the Bible composition, in fact the Church of Rome was instrument in the implementation of them and wholly responsible for the continual propagation of the stories as truth. Those incredible stories demanded from the flock more than a little suspension of any disbelief, and so faith was born. Have faith, believe and all will be well. Do as the Church tells you and you will not spend eternity in a lake of fire. As a control mechanism it has been sensationally successful. The tragedy is that the real truth of spirituality and the teachings of Jesus became buried along the way. The Church, though, didn't mind. They had control of the people.

The following table provides real meanings behind important words in the Bible. I cannot impress on the reader enough the importance of these interpretations. As you read this book you may want to keep referring back to them. You may want to photocopy the page and pass it on to everyone you know. It might just allow them to re-evaluate their lives. Those who do not believe in religion can see immediately that a very different story, a more credible story, emerges: a story that is not full of miracles and impossible events. They will see a spiritual truth that cannot be denied and that at the same time does not demand blind faith from its readers. It is the story of a human spiritual journey that was hijacked by religious fanatics and powerful rulers.

Gone from the equation is sin, that wonderful catch-all that promises eternity in a lake of fire as punishment from a loving God if you don't obey the Church. Gone is the virgin birth. Gone is fable.

Word in Bible	Correct translation
Almah	Often translated as virgin, but actually means young woman.
Babylon	Rome
The lion	Roman emperor Being rescued from the lion's mouth meant escaping the clutches of the emperor or his officers.
The poor	Not poverty-stricken, underprivileged citizens, but those who had been initiated into the higher echelons of the community, and on that account, had been obliged to give up their property and their worldly possessions

Word in Bible	Correct translation
The many	The title used for the head of the celibate community
The crowd	The designation of the regional tetrarch or governor
The multitude	The governing council
The children	Novices within the religious establishment
The Way	The doctrinal theme of the community Those who followed the principles of The Way were known as The Children of Light.
Lepers	Those who had not been initiated into the higher community, or who had been denounced by it In these respects, the healing of a leper refers to the process of conversion to The Way.
The blind	Those who were not party to The Way and could therefore not see 'the light' In these respects, the healing of the blind refers to the process of conversion to The Way.
Raised from the dead	Released from excommunication
Unclean	Uncircumcised gentiles
The sick	Those in public or clerical disgrace
Carpenter	From the Greek *ho hecton* and the semetic word *nagger*, real meaning: craftsman, scholar or teacher Joseph was a high-ranking Essene healer.
Only Son of God	Son only of God
Sin	To miss the mark, to not achieve what you wanted to this time

Word in Bible	Correct translation
Turned water into wine	Similar to 'make a silk purse out of a sow's ear', a saying of the time to mean teaching people The Way
Betray me	Hand me over This is very important when you consider Judas' supposed betrayal of Jesus. This confirms that the handing over was actually planned by Jesus in advance in order that the prophecy of the coming of the Messiah could be fulfilled. Paul did not even meet Jesus until after the crucifixion. *He was not even at the last supper.*

Yet all through my life I have been told that the Bible is the word of God: *add not one word and take not one word away.*

The implications here are enormous. Taking the Bible literally is a colossal mistake that the churches, and in particular the Roman Catholic Church, have ignored. Indeed it appears that although they have expert knowledge of the true meanings, they have done their level best to suppress the true translations outside of the Vatican. The events in the Bible are, in fact, vastly different to that which millions across the world throughout the last two millennia have literally 'taken as gospel'!

Seeking the truth

So what was the truth at the time of Jesus? What exactly did happen and what exactly did he stand for? When was the Bible actually written and by whom? Which religion on Earth, if any, teaches the truth about how we should live our lives, and just why are we here? And why oh why didn't this God of love stop the Hitlers of the world in their tracks?

I decided to investigate further, starting with a quick study of various religions and their associated dogma to try to find any element of truth. I decided too that I would search through history in an attempt to find the real lives of Jesus Christ and his associates. The truth had to be inextricably linked to the Bible misinterpretations and I wanted to find out why the Church had gone on for centuries teaching what they knew to be a lie. What was in it for them that was so good that they ignored the fact that they could lose their very souls – and yet they still did it?

Over the course of the next ten years I devoted my spare time to these endeavours. As I studied and as I dug deeper, over time astonishing truths started to emerge. Like pieces of the same gigantic cosmic jigsaw puzzle, incredibly the pieces started to fit together. Events and consequences thousands of miles and hundreds of years apart began to appear related, eventually being inextricably and undeniably linked.

There is the truth of true spirituality and your undeniable link to the world of spirit, from whence we all came. There is the truth of the real lives of Jesus Christ, Mary Magdalene, John the Baptist and Moses.

And then there is the distorted contrived truth that is religion. This so-called truth is an absolute abomination and a clear insult to Jesus, Mary Magdalene and John the Baptist. You see, the fundamental fact that emerged was that they wanted the real truth of spirituality to spread around the world so that everyone could live life in harmony. But when Christianity arrived and the Bible was composed, it became nothing more than the tool of a controlling, corrupt religion.

The story of the last 2,000 years has been a melting pot of lies, betrayal, secret societies, revenge and – believe it or not – genocide in the name of the Roman Catholic Church – a Church desperate to maintain its status quo, and with it, its position of ultimate power over the lives of millions of followers and devotees. This power is more important to the Church of Rome than any truth that Jesus, Mary and John taught. It will, therefore, ultimately be the Church's downfall.

Notes on the book

Whilst writing the book and talking over the contents of it with many people, I found myself invited to join two 'secret' societies. The truth is not welcome in a world of control. I declined both invitations.

One of the other 'secret' organisations that has played an enormous part in preventing the Roman Catholic Church from permanently destroying this great truth is the Priory of Sion or Our Lady of Zion; in other words, Magdalene. In this book I have made a conscious decision to constantly refer to the Priory in the original 'Zion' although they were and still are more commonly known as 'Sion'. This serves as a reminder that the Priory was formed to guard the secrets of Magdalene.

I have tried to keep to the essence of events, and have not gone into too much detail. The books I recommend for further reading develop the ideas further. And then there are elements that merit further exploration. For instance, throughout my research I found that the date of 17th January continued to crop up as a date on which important things happened over time. Coincidence? Perhaps, who knows – but it strikes me as being more than a little curious.

Although the Church as an institution is vilified by me many times in this little book I do not wish to demean the fantastic work done by those on the 'shop floor' of the various churches.

Any good that is done for fellow creatures is wonderful.

The Church itself, though, teaches and preaches absolute lies and wraps them up in a story parcel labelled 'salvation'. The Church has told its flock for centuries how to live their lives, when to marry and that divorce is a 'sin' against God. It teaches that sex before marriage and homosexuality will earn you an eternity in a lake of fire. It teaches you that faith in Christ alone will ensure your place in heavenly glory. The Roman Catholic Church dictates rules on abortion and contraception, and followers listen and act accordingly, for the views of their pope are the views of God himself – are they not? Well, actually, no, they are not! It disturbs me greatly that countless thousands of loyal Catholics over the centuries have followed the dictates of the Church and lived miserable lives due to loveless marriages because divorce was seen to be a sin against God; that thousands again have been born into poverty because the Church bans contraception or abortion, even after rape. The Church as an institution is monumentally obsessed with its own importance, morally bankrupt and catastrophically flawed. It continually demeans and undermines women and is full of dead men's bones and every kind of corruption.

In the coming pages I will refer a lot to 'God', but my vision of God is nothing like what the Church will have you believe. Only later on in the book will I define 'him' or 'her' with greater clarity.

I hope as you read this book a new world will open up for you. If you are a religious person, I hope you will become enlightened, and if you are agnostic then I hope the truth will inspire you.

The truth is out there

We must start our quest for the truth where I started mine. All through my life I have had many doubts concerning the motives that lie behind the operation of the Churches. How could any Church or 'faith' profess to be divinely ordained and yet feel free to change their doctrine, rules and teachings in order to keep pace with a changing society? Are they merely amending the rules in order to keep up attendances?

Many years ago I asked the question, 'Has the Church got it right? Are they teaching the truth?' After years of sifting and digging the answer has to be a resounding *no*! Never in a billion years could any Church that preaches such doctrines be anywhere near the truth. Any religion that demands subservience through guilt over the death of one man – any man – cannot claim to be associated with a God of love. Any Church or religion that promises an eternity in hellfire and damnation for non-conformists cannot be taken seriously as a promoter of love, forgiveness and divine understanding. 'Ah,' I hear you say, 'but the Church does not demand subservience through guilt over the death of *any* man, it demands it over the death of the son of God.' (But remember that the true interpretation is actually 'son only of God'.)

And even if he were the actual son of God, born to this life as a human being, it beggars belief that a supreme being would send anyone to suffer the way that Jesus did. Was it really so that for the next 2,000 years those who believed in him would be 'saved'? What was this omnipotent, omnipresent and omniscient God thinking of? What about the people all over the world who have never heard of him, the indigenous tribes and those living in remote areas, for instance? What of those who follow Buddha and other faiths, who lead good enlightened lives – are they to be similarly damned? Because make no mistake, if the only way to be 'saved' is to believe in Jesus then all of these peoples are doomed from the moment they are born. If you believe what the Christian faith teaches then only Christians with faith in Jesus are going to heaven. Everyone else might just as well not have been born in the first place. That does not seem to me like the work of a loving God, more of a sadist. In short, the principle stinks. It is without substance and it is a wonder that the Church has got away with this fabrication for so long. It really just is not true. It is a lie!

Don't you think that a true God of love would find a better way to enlighten the peoples of the world to the wonderful ways in which to live life, love and be loved, and exist in true harmony, than to threaten an eternity in hellfire if we do not? You do not throw the baby into the oven just because it has been naughty. And in fact, many of the so-called 'sins' for which you must pray, or ask your priest for forgiveness, are not sins at all in reality. These 'sins' are the invention of the Christian Church in an effort to control lives.

And a classic teaching of the Church is that we are all 'born in sin' and that we bear the sins of our forefathers. *I tell you now that this teaching is wrong*. We are born into this life afresh. I will deal with this issue later, but suffice it to say that we do not come saddled with the 'sins' of our grandparents or anyone else.

When it comes to sins, the Church could not be more wrong.

The sin of sex

The one real affront to God and the natural way is the call to celibacy, the rallying cry of at least one Church institution. Why oh why must a person be celibate in order to be closer to God? What a very strange idea (and one that clearly does not work). Can you imagine what would happen if everyone decided that in order to get closer to God and not be 'corrupted by the flesh' they too would be celibate? The human race would vanish in a lifetime.

The Church has corrupted the act of making love into an abomination. It has told us that the most wonderful God-given gift of love between two people is dirty and disgusting. *But it is not. In fact, it is at the centre of what Jesus and Mary taught. It is the absolute hub of the teachings.* Nature has made the expression of total love such a wonderfully pleasurable experience for two people. It is an expression of real and natural love. But the Church hates it – the Roman Catholic Church actually bans it for their priests!!! In doing this they are actually banning love, the very essence of true spirituality and the core reason for human existence. And this is where the Church has once again gone horribly wrong.

The Christian religion blames the female for the 'fall' of man in the first place in the so-called Garden of Eden. It considers the woman to be the corrupter of man. It tells us that thinking of a female in a sexual way or in a loving way that involves sexual thoughts is wrong and impure. *'Forgive me, Father, for I have sinned – I have had impure thoughts.'* Yet it is the most natural thing in the world for a man to think about a woman this way, and vice-versa of course: It is just as natural for a woman to think of a man in a sexual way also. This is nature after all. Is nature impure? Is nature itself sinful? of course not.

Time and again the Church refers to woman as the *corrupter of man*. But this is the work of a patriarchal institution more fearful of women than anything else. *'To lay with a woman is to lay with corruption itself.'* We will see later that the reverse is the case and that enlightenment is female. The legacy of the Garden of Eden myth as portrayed by the Church fulfils its original intention: The faithful sheep obey.

So, at least one Church bans its priesthood from experiencing what amounts to the epitome of God's works. The Catholic Church bans the priesthood from marrying or becoming involved with a woman in a romantic or sexual way. This denies his workforce of any first-hand experience and knowledge of this type of profound love. It removes the priesthood from any such loving experience – and yet surely God's love is a subject in which the priesthood should be well versed?

The Church, though, believes that making love, the joining of two people in the act of love, is corruption. Unless of course those two people have been joined together in marriage by the Church. So, God's greatest gift to two people only becomes acceptable when the Church gives you the green light and a piece of paper.

Because of the teachings of the Church young girls who became pregnant and were not 'married' were sent away for the duration of the pregnancy in countless numbers to institutions run by Catholic nuns. Parents held the firm belief that their pregnant daughter was a dirty corrupter – a sinner. She was to be sent away before the pregnancy began to show in order that the parents were not shamed in the community. Such was the level of Church-induced stigma that at the very time when a young girl needed her parents most – for help, support and most of all understanding, compassion and love – she was rejected by them at the behest of the Church. In many, many cases these poor unfortunate wretches were treated abominably during their pregnancy incarceration by these representatives of an all-loving God. Directly after giving birth their babies were taken from them. From beginning to end the physical experience was terrible. Add to this the psychological nightmare of being constantly told that you are dirty and unworthy and you have a scenario worthy of a concentration camp. The Church of Rome and its Nazi nuns were as far removed from 'God' as it was possible to be. The young girls – lost, confused, innocent; yes, innocent – received not one scrap of compassion or love.

Marriage is a man-made institution and there is no prerequisite from God that two people who are in love should or should not make love. Making love outside of marriage *is not a sin*. Don't let any priest tell you that it is.

Love is divine. If two people are in love, then nothing is more natural than for them to make love. It is the epitome of a very positive emotion. When there are so many negative emotions like hatred and anger in the world today, the expression of such a positive emotion in such an all-consuming way is pleasing to the spirit world. Marriage is *not* important to God.

Love is what is important to God. To say, as the Church clearly does, that you must get married before you can make love, that no matter what the marriage cannot be dissolved, and that if you do dissolve it you cannot be forgiven is stupidity beyond belief. They impose, then judge, condemn and then outcast. Aren't these *all* the things that Jesus told us *not* to do?

However, let us be perfectly clear on one very important point. Two people who meet and just have sex after only a short while without a deep feeling of love or respect for one another just cheapen themselves and give themselves too freely. They should really wait for that special person for true love to be involved. Not waiting, though, is no sin before God, but it can affect self-esteem. All I would really say is choose your partners as wisely as you can. Only sleep with those you love. Be as sure as you can be before you give everything. Then *love* and don't feel guilty about it – feel good.

I am so glad that some rules have been relaxed as the Church struggles to come to terms with modern life. Dogma, rules, intransigence and then, when it suits them, a rethink! Such institutions are doomed to fail. And it is because they teach not the truth but only control. If what they were teaching, preaching and imposing on their 'flocks' was correct before then a relaxing of the rules or a rethink according to life situations would not be possible. Truth cannot be amended. Truth stands forever.

Homosexuality

So what else is wrong with the Church? Let us take a look at another thorny issue, that of homosexuality. Countless hours of debate have ensued, dozens of books have been written and the Church is totally incapable of handling the matter, for it is as far away from God on this issue as it is with so many others. The Church outlaws homosexuality outright and its members practise it – many, no doubt, because they have been forbidden to marry or be with a woman with all the experiences of true love attached to that.

Politicians fight shy of the issue. The Church buries all its perceived love and compassion in the nearest bunker and comes down hard against anyone who dare admit to being homosexual. Another huge mistake. More condemning and no compassion.

The fact is that homosexuality exists. It is not to be feared or condemned. It is nothing more than one of nature's twists and is not something to be judged or questioned.

The problem for today's society is that the Church has been completely incompetent in leading the way on how homosexuality is perceived. The early Church, at the time of the Bible writers, outlawed homosexuality outright, making it difficult, if not impossible, for any loving, understanding Church to embrace it. The stupidity of the Church has caused the population to hate and fear gay people; because their love is different, it is ridiculed and condemned.

Perhaps we should look more closely at the Native American view of the homosexual person, a far more enlightened viewpoint than anything you could garner from a visit to your local priest or vicar (that fact alone speaks volumes). In Native American spirituality the homosexual was regarded as a special person for he/she was a mixture of both sexes. He/she was two people in one body. He/she was consulted on many issues that may affect the tribe. He/she was considered to be able to see the problem from two different aspects. He/she had a greater level of understanding. He/she was blessed with both the male and female viewpoint. When sitting in council and agreement could not be reached on a problem affecting the whole tribe, the special person was called upon for his/her view.

What a wonderfully positive way of looking at it. Isn't it such a pity that our 'civilised' society should, for most of the time, be so negative? And it is the teachings of the Church and its innate inability to see the positive that has propagated this negativity.

Circumcision

Some Churches practise circumcision. Circumcision of either the male or female baby is nothing short of barbaric. It is mutilation of the body that nature has provided. What is it about man that makes him think that he knows better than Mother Nature what form the body should or should not take? The barbarism is compounded by the fact that it is merely a religious matter, and to be true to your religion the circumcision is vital. More rules made by man, and this time it ends in agony for tiny babies. Barbaric – wrong, wrong, wrong!

Disempowering the female

Right from the start and the Garden of Eden, the Bible portrays the female as the villain. She is the corrupter of man! Make no mistake: our patriarchal Churches have fun demeaning and blaming the female. Yet who stood below the cross to support Jesus when the so-called blessed rock Peter and the divine Paul had denied Jesus and fled into the darkness like scurrying rats? The females stood by him: Mary, his mother; Mary Magdalene; and her sister Martha. In the New Testament we see phrases like 'keep your women silent in Church'. And does it not seem strange that we have a male Holy Trinity? God the Father, God the Son, God the Holy Ghost. A clear agenda is evident to all readers: that women are 'unworthy'. But this teaching is clearly wrong. It is just another part of the dogma of lies.

Women priests is another thorny issue for the Church as it struggles to control an ever more enlightened flock. Women priests are a wholly good idea. When Jesus was asked by his disciples why it was that he let Mary Magdalene speak, he replied: 'Whoever shall preach the word of God is divinely ordained to speak.' There is nothing ambiguous about that statement.

Is it not a little strange that the modern Churches appear to have forgotten this as members struggle to keep female vicars out? The Bible says 'keep your women silent in Church', but this is clearly against Jesus' teachings and all that he knew. They are the words of Paul, who we know to be a woman hater. We also know that both Paul and Peter were against women because they felt threatened by the high esteem in which Jesus held Mary Magdalene. The thoughts and words of Paul and Peter have been responsible for almost all Western Churches treating women with contempt.

In some areas Muslim women are not allowed to be educated or even learn to drive. They are not allowed to show their faces in public and are totally subservient to their men. Since biblical times women have been regarded as second-class citizens, only gaining the vote in England, for example, at the beginning of the 20th century. The Church, though, still objects to female priests and many churches vehemently refuse to have a female 'vicar in charge'.

Peter and Paul's legacy of stupidity and ignorance goes on.

In *The Templar Revelation* authors Lynn Picknett and Clive Prince state that:

> It is clear from the way that [Mary Magdalene] is mentioned that she was the most important of all Jesus' female disciples, all of whom are almost totally ignored by the Church. First century Jews may have had sociological and religious problems with the concept of important women, simply because of their culture, more recent critics have no excuse.
>
> During the never-ending arguments about women priests, extraordinary misrepresentations of Jesus' followers were cited

as proof that women were not meant to be members of the clergy.

I will deal with Jesus' relationship with Mary Magdalene later, but suffice it to say that it was the insecurity of Jesus' male disciples, so threatened did they feel by the presence of the Magdalene as a disciple, that led them to be derisory toward women as a whole.

This situation was made entirely worse by Pope Gregory I in the relatively early days of the Roman Catholic Church who declared that as the Gospel of Luke had stated that Magdalene had 'had seven demons cast out of her', she must have 'perfumed her flesh with forbidden acts'. Since that time the Church has depicted her as a prostitute. As Lynn Picknett says in her excellent book, *Mary Magdalene – Christianity's Hidden Goddess*:

Only in 1969 did the Roman Catholic Church repeal Gregory's labelling of Mary as a whore, thereby admitting their error. Though the image of Mary Magdalene as a penitent whore has remained in the public teachings of all Christian denominations. Like a small erratum buried in the back pages of a newspaper, the Church's correction goes unnoticed, while the initially incorrect defamatory article continues to influence readers.

The Oxford English Dictionary defines Magdalene as 'penitent whore'; another legacy, then, of a corrupt Catholic Church.

Corruption

In his book *The Last Pope* John Hogue details many of the institution's transgressions, some more heinous than others. One story, concerning the death of John Paul I, he details as follows:

> John Paul was determined to examine the Vatican's financial affairs. Since 1974 the former patriarch of Venice had been following news reports suggesting that the Vatican bank was being used as a front for criminal behaviour. The relatively young institution had been founded by Pius X1 after he and Benito Mussolini agreed to establish the Vatican City-State through the Lateran Treaty of 1929. Pope Paul [VI] had chosen an old friend Michele Sidona – a Sicilian banker with close ties to the Mafia and neo-fascist organisations – as a financial advisor to the Vatican Bank. Sidona, in the coming years, would draw the financial lifeblood of the Church's flush coffers to support a huge network of money laundering, corruption, murder and fraud.

> John Paul was aware of these accusations and he voiced his desire to Villot that an investigation be made. He also indicated his readiness, if need be, to relocate several Vatican insiders who were major players in the operations known as Vatican Inc.

No doubt his investigations would have uncovered the Vatican connections with the Mafia and with the right wing Freemasons group known as P2. But before he could set the plans for his investigation in motion, Pope John Paul 1st died from a heart attack.

The night before the Pope planned to start his reformation of the Vatican bank and make changes to key posts, he retired to bed at 9-30pm. His servants found him at 4-45am, dead in his bed, with his papers listing who was to be dismissed scattered over the covers and the floor. As soon as Cardinal Villot was summoned to the bedroom he pocketed the papers, along with the Pope's last will and testament (which had been on his desk in his study). John Paul always had a bottle of Effortil at his bedside to regulate his low blood pressure.

Witnesses testified that Cardinal Villot had the bottle immediately cleared from the bedroom. Then he issued false statements to the police and the press about the circumstances surrounding the death of the Pope. The controversial list has never been publicly disclosed. In Florence, Cardinal Benelli emerged for a press conference on the morning the Pope's death was announced. With tears in his eyes he said; 'The Church has lost the right man for the right moment. We are very distressed. We are left frightened.'

Villot's suspicious behaviour immediately attracted the press, who clamoured for an autopsy. Villot declined, giving the excuse that there was no precedent for such a request. He either did not know – or did not want the press to know – that an autopsy had been performed on Clement X1V back in 1775. Before anyone could counter his objection, Villot had the Pope's body carried off to the Vatican coroners to be embalmed. To this day the Vatican angrily denies foul play.

This is what Jesus was talking about when he said, 'Like whitened sepulchres; on the outside pure and white and on the inside, full of dead men's bones and every kind of corruption.' Nothing has changed in the temples since he was alive!

The Church, then, is inept, incompetent and a control freak. Compare this to Native American spirituality.

Native American spirituality

Before the invasion of America by the Europeans, the Native American tribes were spread across this great land. Wildlife was plentiful, and natural food from trees, bushes and plants was in abundance.

The Native American people were exceptionally spiritual. They realised that they were part of nature, that they were but a single strand in the entire and complex web of life. They loved and appreciated all that was around them, for all of nature was a part of Great Spirit. Everything lived in spirit, the four-leggeds, the trees (the Indians called them 'the standing people'), the plants, the rocks, the rainbows and the Earth itself. They took from nature only what they needed to live and nothing more. Nature and all of her creatures and plants were appreciated and respected. Before cutting down a tree they prayed to the spirit of the tree to allow itself to be used. Before killing an animal they prayed to the spirit of the animal, that it may give itself to them and return once more to spirit. Once killed, they prayed to Great Spirit to love and receive the spirit of the animal.

They wasted no part of the animal for it had given its life for them. They ate as much of it as they could. They used the skin for clothing and for tepee building. They used the bone for ceremonies and for personal adornment. The people of Turtle Island positively revered the children and the elderly of the tribes: the children because they had only recently come from spirit and as such were closer to it, and the elderly because they had lived full lives and had much wisdom to impart and they were close to returning to spirit. The elderly or older members of the tribe traditionally looked after the children while the mothers were away fruit and berry gathering and the fathers were away hunting. The tribes considered this to be in keeping with Great Spirit, for the old ones had a lifetime of experiences and knowledge to impart to the young ones. Plus they were preparing to return to Great Spirit and would instil in the youngsters all the wisdom that they had accumulated over their lifetime.

With regard to the females, whilst the men purified their bodies and their spirit also, by sitting in the sweat lodge for long hours and possibly days, the women did not. It was considered that Mother Nature purified the women with the menstrual cycle. This not only made them closer to Mother Earth but it also meant that they were naturally purer than the male. If during council, when important matters were discussed, a woman wanted to speak, she was always listened to intently for she was female, as is nature herself. Woman's love knows no bounds. She is the bearer and nurturer of new life and her wisdom is great.

It is interesting to note that when the Native Americans sat in council they left their tomahawks in the ground outside the tepee. This would allow them to talk things over spiritually with everyone who came from other tribes without other disputes getting in the way. It is where we get our saying 'bury the hatchet'.

When the white man arrived in America there were 60 million buffalo roaming the Great Plains. By 1860 there were less than 200 animals. The white man knew that the Native American depended on the buffalo for food and clothing, so in order to exterminate the Native American, first you had to cut off his supply of food. By the time the Native American wars were in full swing, with cavalry generals proclaiming that the only good 'Indian' was a dead one, the railroads ran special trains across the plains full of men with rifles to shoot as many buffalo as possible along the way. Where they fell, they were left to rot. This wanton slaughter was never understood by the red man. To kill in this way was against every law of nature.

Similarly, the red man could not understand the wholesale forest clearing that was going on. 'Why do you take away the trees that have stood for so long? Without the trees the land will become barren.' The white man did not listen. Now the USA is without 75 per cent of its topsoil. The white man lied, made false treaties with the Native Americans, took their lands by force, confined them to barren reservations to starve, provided them with small-pox-ridden blankets, and mutilated, raped and murdered their women and children.

Then the white man wanted the 'savage' to convert to Christianity.

Chief White Cloud said:

> Your religious calling was written on plates of stone, by the flaming finger of an angry God. Our religion was established

by the traditions of our ancestors, the dreams of our elders that are given to them in the silent hours of the night by Great Spirit, and the premonitions of the learned beings. It is written in the hearts of our people, thus, we do not need Churches, which would only lead us to argue over God. And the thought that white men should rule over nature and change its laws according to his liking, was never understood by the red man. Our belief is that Great Spirit created all things, not just mankind, but all animals, rocks and plants, all on Earth and amongst the stars, with true soul. For us – all life is holy. But you do not understand our prayers when we address the sun, the moon, the winds. You have judged us without understanding – only because our prayers are different. But we are able to live in harmony with all of nature. All of nature is within us and we are all part of nature.

Man has a poor understanding of life. He mistakes knowledge for wisdom. He tries to unveil the Holy secrets of our father, Great Spirit. He attempts to impose his laws and ways on Mother Earth, even though he himself is a part of nature, he chooses to disregard and ignore it for the sake of his own immediate gain. But the laws of nature are far stronger than those of mankind. Man must awake at last and learn to understand how little time there remains before he will become the cause of his own downfall. And he has much to learn, to learn to see with his heart.

He must learn to respect Mother Earth, she who has given life to everything, to our brothers and sisters, the animals, the plants, to the rivers, the lakes, the oceans and the winds. He must realise that the planet does not belong to him but that he has to care for and maintain the delicate balance of nature, for the sake of the wellbeing of our children and all future generations. It is the duty of man to preserve the Earth and the creation of the Great Spirit, mankind being but a grain of sand in the Holy circle which encloses all life.

Cree Indian philosophy:

Only after the last tree has been cut down

Only after the last fish has been caught

Only after the last river has been poisoned

Only then will you find that money cannot be eaten.

And finally the view of the Native Americans to whom the idea of original sin and 'sinful nature' was incomprehensible. taken from Wa Na Nee Che and Timothy Freke's book *Native American Spirituality*:

They could not understand a God who was hateful and vengeful and delights in setting humans up with temptation and then punishing them when they succumb. Similarly they thought it quite odd that our religious leaders said that if a person performed a ritual prescribed by a priest, their God would be induced to forget about their having committed murder, theft or rape. 'Wouldn't this allow bad behaviour?' They asked. The whole idea of a God whose primary function was to be a book-keeper but a forgetful one was incomprehensible to them.

Death: the most natural of occurrences – so why fear it?

We fear death in large part thanks to the Church. They preach hellfire and damnation, a lake of fire awaits. We dress in black for funerals, we mourn, we weep and we cannot imagine life without our loved ones. No wonder, then, that death is so feared. Most people standing at the graveside still are not sure about life after death, even those firm followers of the Church and members of a particular flock. The doubt is there.

At the graveside there are those who do not believe in God and an afterlife at all. They are just paying their last respects and going through the motions of the service. The religious service means nothing to them. The person has died and that is that. Gone forever.

Then there are those who believe in the teachings of the Church. These are the ones who hope above hope that their friend, loved one or acquaintance will not go to hell but instead spend an eternity in heaven. There seems little hope, though: the Church has made it pretty inevitable that we are all destined for the other place. So many rules – so impossible to follow.

So let us ask the question: At the point of death when the body ceases to function, is that it? Do we just cease to be? The look of the body certainly seems to bear this out. It is but an empty shell – all life extinguished forever. It is placed into the ground to rot or cremated. You will never see that body again. It is pretty final. All the dressing in black and the wailing does not help. And all the Church can say by way of hope is, 'Well, we hope he/she has gone to heaven.' Very reassuring, I'm sure!

It sometimes appears to me that the people who don't believe in life after death at all are better equipped to deal with death and funerals. After all, although probably equally upset at the time, at least they don't have to worry about the possibility of their friend or relative suffering for eternity in a lake of fire. It is certainly ironic that an eternity dead is preferable to an eternity of hellfire at the hands of a loving God!

Many people who don't believe in life after death have never studied the subject at all. Caught up in the materialistic here and now, they say that this is as good as it gets and when you die that's it. And you can't really blame them. With all of the hypocrisy and lies of religion it is little wonder that so many more people are turning their backs on it.

I once witnessed a 45-year-old woman tell her 85-year-old father, 'Don't talk like that, Dad – you'll go to hell!' And she was deadly serious.

Let me state quite decisively that when we die we return to the world of spirit from whence we came. The teachings of the Church regarding heaven and hell are quite fictitious. There is no such place as heaven and no such place as hell. The only hell is in your own mind when you realise that you did not improve your spirit in the way that you wanted to when you chose to return to this life. But it is more of a deep regret and disappointment. Not at all like the place threatened by the Church of love.

Let us look at what really happens and leave religion to its stories and fables.

In her excellent book *Between Death and Life* Dolores Cannon has recorded account of subjects she has regressed to a previous life and through the death experience. What her subjects talked of is fascinating and awe-inspiring. None of her regression subjects knew each other and the regressions were recorded over many years. The spirits with whom Dolores conversed in this way really appear to be trying to emphasise that it is the philosophical dogma that forms part of religious institutions that prevents people from being able to comprehend what is the truth of the spiritual realm. One of the principle stumbling blocks in the Christian religion is the teaching that each soul only has one incarnation, the idea that you only have one shot at getting it right - only one attempt and then its either heaven or hell for you. The concept is foolish say the spirits, and they wonder why people on this earth walk even contemplate the idea! They ask: 'Is it any harder to believe that you can be born once into a body, than to believe that you can be born twice or more?'

Many of the Churches do not want people to believe in prior or successive existences because it loosens their grip of fear and they no longer have control. The leaders of great schools of thought knew of previous existence and successive existence but it was closed off to general knowledge by those in power because of the need to control people.

In other hypnotic regressions spirits talk of the many lives we have lived and of those yet to live. They tell us that we return to live an earthly life purely to improve our spirit, to become a more enlightened spirit, to eventually acquire ultimate spirituality. They tell of the harm done by the Church in the promises of hellfire. Continually the spirits talk of the Church's wrongful control over the people and the many teachings of the ancient world lost and ignored by the Church. They speak of the dawning of a new age and they state that the truth will surface and return in the new age. This is the dawning of the Age of Aquarius. It is time that we were all enlightened.

In one regression Dolores finds herself talking to an old woman who is about to go through the death experience. Her body was old, tired and she obviously endured more than her fair share of aches and pains. Just moving was around was hard for her so Dolores moved her forward to a point just beyond the death experience.

The following is an extract from Between Death & Life by Dolores Cannon.

D = Dolores

S = Spirit

    D   Can you see the body?

    S   (Disgusted) Ohh! That old thing? It's down there! Ohh! I had no idea I looked so bad! I was so wrinkled and shrivelled. I feel too good to be that shrivelled! It was all wore out. (she was making sounds of delight) Oh Oh I'm so glad I'm here!

D   No wonder it was shrivelled, that body lived many years. That's probably why it died. You said you were 'here' where are you?

S   I'm in the light, and oooh, it feels good! I feel intelligent… I feel peace… I feel calm. I don't need anything.

It continues and becomes even more enlightening.

And now let me state quite categorically that you should not fear death for we have done it many times. There is no pain in death, in the soul leaving the physical body. The transition is one of ease rather than duress. Whatever pain the body is experiencing at the time of death is completely removed as you pass over. The process is very easy and natural. There are feelings of release and a feeling of great love envelops you. You are assured and calm. One spirit said, 'Dying is pleasant. If people are worried about it, tell them to go to a place in a river that has a deep pool. Tell them to dive to the bottom of the pool. Then, at the bottom, push up vigorously with their feet and come plunging to the surface. Tell them that it is like that.'

There are no such places as heaven and hell as portrayed by the Church, but in the world of spirit there is peace, love and a truly magical realm. No harps and clouds forever, that would be boring after a while! But life in spirit is ongoing, always with purpose, always progressing and evolving. With spiritual evolvement comes other planets, other universes, other spirits on materialistic journeys of many forms who need help – just as we do now.

We must all understand that this life we are living now is one of many we have lived; some have reincarnated over 100 times. When viewed from this perspective it is easy to see how death should not be feared. When *you* decided to come on this incarnation, you did so to improve your spirit by gaining more enlightenment. Maybe in your last incarnation there was a particular problem that you could not or did not face and you chose to return and experience it again. We all wish to be close to the creator, the Great Spirit of Native American culture, God of the Christian religion, call him or her what you will.

There are those who have walked the Earth who have come to us from a higher spiritual plane, those who are very great spiritual entities, those who are really enlightened who veritably ooze positive energy. They reincarnate to help. People like Jesus Christ and the Buddha are but two of these. This subject is covered in depth in the book referred to above and I urge you to read it for it contains the truth.

'The light came into the world but men prefer darkness' is a quote from the Bible that many if not all of us have heard. Yet how close to the truth is that statement?

Imagine, if you will, that the world of spirit has nine very distinct and separate levels. Imagine (in its simplest form) that spirits inhabit these levels and the lowest level is the spirit furthest away from the creator, the light. It is an unenlightened spirit, one with much to learn and experience in order to fulfil and become closer to the creator. It is not an evil spirit for there is no such thing. *There is no such thing as good and bad spirits – only evolving spirits.* In some instances it is merely a spirit with lots of negative karma, and in some it is a spirit with many experiences yet to go through. Both have much to learn and much to achieve. It naturally follows, then, that those on the upper levels are close to Great Spirit and are full of positive energy, compassion, wisdom and, of course, love.

Life on Earth is all about spiritual enlightenment. That is why it is imperative not to get too involved with the love of material things and the world's wealth, for that will inevitably all pass from us. You *will* leave it all behind. No matter how much money you make and how many houses, boats and cars you own, these will mean nothing to you when you return to spirit. These are not achievements that mean anything at all to the improvement of your spirit or karma. What is important and will be important to you is what went on in your heart at every decision-making moment in your life. How many people have you hurt with the decisions you made? How many people did you help with the decisions that you made? How many people and animals and even plants of the Earth are spiritually better off for you having touched their lives?

We should all know in our hearts the right thing to do, every minute of every day, at every decision-making moment in our lives. We should all know when something is the wrong thing to do, if it will hurt someone in some way, if it is against Mother Nature or when it would cause any person, animal or plant any suffering or hurt.

Unfortunately many people in the world today have lost their spiritual way. They appear to be driven by greed for the wealth of the world. This is, sadly, the fault of the culture that we are all born into, and the nurture that we receive. True spirituality was lost to the world 2,000 years ago. What we have left now, as an alternative to living a materialistic life, is an organised and controlling religion, itself flawed and broken. So it is that many people are so busy just living their lives that they don't even consider asking the question *why* they are living this life. Many people live life only to 'get on', and that means more money, a bigger house, more cars. The tragedy is that this is seen as the right course of action to achieve a fulfilling life. This will make your life complete. We now live in a society of greed, financial ambition and self-interest. The way of spirituality is lost. We are living our lives so desperately 'out of balance' with nature and the spiritual world.

What this society creates is those who have the 'good' life and those who do not. Those who have the 'good' life do not care about those who do not. 'That's their fault.' The result is theft, rape, muggings, murder and a total inability for humans to get on together. Sometimes a person is attacked just because he or she is wearing a label that the other person wants. Society teaches that possession of this is good, and to be seen as a worthwhile person this is the item that you must possess and be seen to possess. In recent years particularly the human mind has become exceptionally shallow, and it will get worse before it gets better. Human beings today, then, are very materialistic. They have lost the way of spirit. The end result will be that the fabric of society will start to fall apart.

True wisdom is the gift of knowing that we are all part of nature, knowing that we are not human beings on a spiritual journey but *spiritual beings on a human journey*. When Jesus said that it was easier for a camel to go through the eye of a needle than for a rich man to enter the kingdom of heaven, the man he was talking to walked away. Given the choice of his money or spiritual enlightenment, he chose his money. Jesus could just as easily have been talking to many people alive today. So consumed with life, cars, promotion at work, houses, holidays, there is no time for spiritual thinking. But if tragedy strikes the family, the death of a loved one perhaps, then the world of materialism falls apart. It is like a sudden and brutal wake-up call and it should bring home to anyone the futility of the rat race; mostly, though, it does not. And for those who do wake up, the feelings are usually short-lived.

This religion, with its theme of subservience through guilt and stories of hellfire, must fall.

People look to vicars and priests for answers to questions like 'Why did my son/daughter have to die so young?' or 'Why did Dad have to suffer so horribly in his later years?' or 'Why did my little boy die of disease at only eight years old – what had he done to offend God?'. The Church has no answer for grieving families apart from 'It's all part of God's wonderful plan for us' or 'Maybe he suffered for something his ancestors did'. These kind of statements offer no comfort at all and merely represent the ramblings of a religion lost for so long in its own dogma that it really hasn't a clue.

Gradually, the controlling Church will lose its grip on people as they question more and more the inconsistencies and the massive black holes in the various dogmas. At this point the population will either go entirely materialistic, with disastrous consequences, or the teachings of true spirituality will surface and prevail. True spirituality must endure.

It is important to remember that when we do return to this life we are born into it with no knowledge of the spirit world that we just left behind. We have no prior knowledge of why we are here and what we should be doing. This life should be a mystery, otherwise if we knew for certain that there was life after death and that it was good, we would rush to commit suicide as soon as life threw us any real problems or misfortunes. This is a very important fact and one that is crucial to the whole spiritual fulfilment exercise. In this life we must have freedom of choice in all things we do in order to grow spiritually, to do the right thing every minute of every day because we want to. Because we know it is the right thing to do and we do it no matter what the cost to us in this life. It is what goes on in our hearts that is important. It is not only what we do, *it is why we do it that counts.* Definite knowledge of the spirit world would remove free will.

The rich man may give a few thousand pounds to charity and then go to Church on a Sunday seeking forgiveness for his 'sins' while his employees cut down the rainforests and rape the planet. The Catholic Church will say that his 'sins' are forgiven. This is simply incredulous and an example of the high esteem in which the Catholic Church holds itself.

The Catholic taking of confession and absolving of sins is spiritually worthless, has no substance and is totally irrelevant.

Successive popes through the ages have always made forgiveness of sins a saleable item to help swell the Vatican coffers during hard times for the Church. This practice has removed any vestige of credibility the Church might have claimed. It even 'sold' guaranteed places in heaven to the rich when times were really bad!

As John Hogue explains in his book *The Last Pope* concerning Pope John XXII:

> Any sin could be forgiven by this Pope if the sinner offered the right price. He even encouraged Catholics to sin again, or break their vows, as long as they could pay for continued forgiveness. It seemed that the biggest sin was being in arrears with the pontiff. In one day John excommunicated 1 Patriarch, 5 Archbishops, 30 Bishops and 46 Abbots for not paying their taxes to the church on time!

The Church is not the one who has to forgive, and neither is God: You will only deal with yourself when you return to spirit. Only you will deal with your actions during this lifetime and you will either feel that you have succeeded spiritually – or that you have not.

The giving of money to charity may ease the conscience on Earth but it will do nothing to ease his soul's disappointment and sense of failure upon its return to spirit.

You see, the man eased his conscience with his charitable donation, yet in his heart he knew he was still engaged in cutting down the rainforests, hurting animals, and the like. He will only realise his failure when he returns to spirit for there is no judgement of you, except *by you*; and no forgiveness for you – except by you – when you return to spirit. You and only you will consider whether or not you have failed in this life. And you will *know* if you have. For, once there, you are indeed a deeply spiritual creature once again and will be painfully aware of your failings during your earth walk.

That is a measure of the distance between the Church and spirituality.

This earthly body that we inhabit is a gift from nature to use whilst we are here and we should look after it. When we are done with it, it will either be burned or returned to the Earth in a ceremony by the people we leave behind. Their grief is a very personal one. I have never been able to understand the people who believe in life after death in the normal Church way, who weep and wail constantly at funerals and for some time after.

If only the truth that Jesus tried to teach, which many people are trying to impart now, was known to all, we would not grieve for loved ones. We would be sad, of course, that we would not see them again for some time, but we would celebrate their life. We would be sure and certain that we would meet them again when we, like them, return to spirit. But the Church with its teachings of hellfire and damnation makes death such a terrible thing, a thing to be feared. Some religions even believe that the dead sleep until the judgement day, when God will appear and judge everyone for everything: *one life, one chance, then judgement.* I'm glad to say that is definitely *just not true.*

Tangible proof of life after death is non-existent and must remain so. The evidence is all around us, though, for those who seek it (auras, vision quests, healers, mediums, clairvoyants etc.). 'Those who have eyes to see, let them see,' said Jesus.

With no proof or first-hand knowledge of life after death it's up to you.

The Church teaches that Jesus Christ said: 'No one shall come to the Father but by me.' He did not say that exactly, but this phrase in its present form has allowed the Church to state that only if you go to Church can you get your ticket to heaven! That is just not so. God/Great Spirit, this massive, positive energy force that surges through the universe, is within us all, for we are all made of energy.

When we die the body dies and returns to the Earth for it is part of the Earth, but the spirit, the life force energy, goes on. You will note that I just said *when we die*. But it is just the body that dies. It is material and grows old – its component parts wear out and malfunction until eventually this earthly body that we inhabit whilst we are here just cannot function any longer. At that point it dies. The heart stops – all bodily functions cease – and the spirit, the energy force that is our essence, leaves that body behind and returns to spirit.

When you leave this life and return to spirit you will be greeted and comforted and you will assess the life you have led. You will decide, with your guides, whether or not you have achieved in that life the enlightenment and progression that you wanted to achieve. When living this life it is how you deal with your life situations that can affect your karma or spirit in either a positive or negative way.

To sum it all up, you must not fear death. You must remember that *you chose this life* and the family that you would be born into. Your spirit guides have been with you all of your life and are with you now.

At the moment of death, whether you are old, your body twisted, or whether you are young, diseased, or die horribly, you will be released from all pain, released from all restrictions imposed by an ageing body, and you will be euphoric. You will be greeted by loved ones and guides, and over a period of time you will assess your life and decide whether or not you accomplished all that you had set yourself to do when you decided to live that life. Has your spirit improved in quality and light? Have you learned more of love, consideration, compassion or any particular lesson that you had chosen that life for?

The fundamental fact for all of us to learn here and now is that each of us is in control of our own destiny. The Church is not in control of you, nor can it ever be. It cannot forgive 'sins', and many so-called 'sins' are not sins at all. But most of all, the Church does not teach the truth. It alone will go down in history as the perpetrator of the biggest lie ever told and believed. It alone is responsible for so many people losing their way spiritually. It alone is responsible for riddling people's lives with lies concerning Jesus Christ and his 'mission' on Earth.

The Church alone has sought to control people en masse and taken out terrible retribution on so-called 'heretics' who do not obey or have the audacity to hold a different opinion. Mass burnings, torture and rape across the land and all in the name of a loving God. It is a wonder so many people still blindly follow, but they do!

Going back to the roots

If the Church has perpetrated this lie for so long, then where has the truth been buried, and at what point in time did it all go horribly wrong for mankind?

We must return to a time when the truth about our life on Earth was about to be brought to us again. We must go back 12,500 years for this truth. It is a truth that has survived despite the best efforts of successive pharaohs, modern Egyptologists, the Roman Catholic Church and political leaders. All have had a vested interest in concealing the truth. The pharaohs lied mostly because they believed themselves to be God incarnate. Egyptologists tell lies concerning the dating of the Sphinx and the Pyramids; for some reason they refuse to accept professional scientific advice that tells them otherwise. And the Sphinx and the Pyramids are exceptionally important in all of this.

The Churches have propagated the biggest lie in the history of mankind: that Jesus was the son of God and that he died on the cross for your 'sins'. In their single-minded determination to control the people they have inflicted unimaginable harm of hundreds of millions of souls. That is the real cost of their lies and deceit.

Now the search for the truth is over. You will have to suspend your earthly materialistic teachings and your scepticism concerning life on other planets and past civilisations on Earth, for everything in nature and the universe is part of the greater picture, each a component part of an enormous tapestry.

Scepticism is what keeps people blinkered to the truth and ties them to the social conditioning to which they have been subjected all their life.

But open your eyes and your mind to the infinite possibilities of the universe and try to put into context your narrow materialistic and sceptical existence. The facts that I am about to give you are real. Whether you believe them or not is entirely up to you. It is your spirituality. What I am about to convey to you may seem incredible, but it is an astonishing truth. It is the essence of Jesus' true teachings and the subject of 2,000 years of incredible intrigue, murder, betrayal and secret societies.

Someone once said to me that the mind is like a parachute – it works better when it's open. So open your mind to the wondrous events that happened so long ago and have been buried for so long since. Open your mind to the indisputable facts of the real lives of Jesus, Mary Magdalene and John. Learn what really happened after the crucifixion and see how people since the time of Jesus, like the Knights Templar, Leonardo Da Vinci and even Nostradamus, have played such important roles in preserving the truth across the centuries.

First we must take a look at the real lives of Jesus, Mary Magdalene, John, Martha, Lazarus, Joseph and Mary (Jesus' mother). It is a story far removed from that told by the Church and believed by millions. It is a very significant part of a 12,500-year evolving story.

Because by the time Jesus became involved the story was already 10,500 years in the making.

Jesus, High Priestess Mary Magdalene and the Temple of Isis

Two thousand years ago Egypt was just about at the centre of the known world. Jesus was born into a world that was ruled by Romans and they were not very popular. Jesus' father Joseph was a teacher, not a carpenter. He was an Essene healer. Remember, this is another Bible error (see the table on page xx). The Essenes (from the Greek *Essenoi* – meaning physician) were a reasonably close-knit community based at Qumran. They were accomplished healers and worked with great knowledge to heal the sick from far and wide. They practised herbal medicine, producing their own ointments and medicines from plants traded from across the Mediterranean. The Essenes were the only peoples to dress almost entirely in white, a tradition maintained to this day by doctors the world over, and whenever they travelled to other communities they were instantly recognised by that white apparel and called upon to heal. They were also very spiritual people. They were students of Isis and the astronomer priests from Heliopolis in Egypt.

(It is worthy of note here that the 'beloved disciple' John Mark was a specialist also in curative healing and remedial medicine, attached to the Egyptian Therapeutate [relative in name with the English; therapeutic]. John Mark was the one to whom Jesus entrusted his mother at the crucifixion.)

Jesus was born to Mary and Joseph, not by any divine intervention or 'immaculate conception' but in the normal manner. There has been much speculation among scholars in recent years concerning Mary's 'status' and the considered opinion (from remaining evidence) seems to be that she did indeed conceive Jesus 'out of wedlock', and to save her honour Joseph married her. There appears to be some evidence that Jesus' father was in fact a Roman centurion but the truth is somewhat different, although I can see where the confusion would originate.

Mary was a fairly normal girl who lived a modest and quiet life with loving parents. But Mary was a striking beauty and one thing really concerned her: her parents had in mind that she should marry a Roman centurion named Quintus. Quintus was hopelessly in love with Mary, this vision of loveliness, this quiet, unassuming creature, and called upon her regularly. Mary, though, would have none of it. She was restless. She used to wander for hours alone in the quiet areas of scrub just outside of her village, day after day, alone with her thoughts on life and contemplating the world and life and all its complexities.

And it was on one of these days when she was wandering the wilderness through the sand and grassy banks that she met a man. He was a man unlike any other she had known or met before, a man who appeared to be everything. He had answers to Mary's myriad of questions about life and what it is all about, the things you should do and the things you should not. He was not only wise but strikingly handsome. Mary fell for him hopelessly and completely.

Mary met and talked with him many times over the course of many weeks, same place, same time. They would spend hours sitting on a small, sandy hill just talking, and eventually, as love grew, cuddling also. Mary knew that this was the man she wanted to be with, this was the man she wanted to lay with. But this man was somewhat strange, deliciously different in a spiritual kind of way and yet something about him was not quite right. Mary could sense it but she put it to the back of her mind for this was the man she was in love with.

Over the coming months the inevitable happened and Mary fell pregnant. All this time the centurion Quintus was still pursuing her, captivated as he was by her beauty. But Mary was in trouble – deep trouble. The day she chose to meet the man she loved to tell him that she was with child, he did not show up.

Distraught beyond belief, after a few weeks, when Mary began to show, she told her parents of the man, whose name she did not even know, and the times they had spent together. When he heard of Mary's predicament from her mother, Quintus left, never to be seen by Mary again.

Mary knew Joseph quite well. He was an Essene and a healer and Mary had noticed him watching as she wandered off to meet her man in the valley outside the settlement day after day. She had never considered him as a potential partner for he was much older than her. But he realised that she was with child and without the man she had loved. He could see the pain on her face as the days passed and he knew that she would be an outcast in the community before too long. So Joseph proposed marriage. He wanted to marry Mary because he admired her, he appreciated her beauty and he wanted to save her from the culture of the day that would surely persecute her.

So Joseph did indeed marry Mary. But who was this man whom nobody but Mary ever saw, to whom Mary gave so much and yet did not even know his name, this man so wise in the ways of spirituality? It was as if he existed only for Mary – and then he was gone. He was gone at the time, it could be argued, that Mary needed him the most.

The Mary depicted in the Bible is a very different Mary – a girl plucked from obscurity by God to be blessed by him planting 'his seed' inside her. Mary, it seems, is no more than a tool in God's toolbox; an instrument used to achieve a particular outcome. The truth is rather different.

The 'Virgin birth' scenario was, however, one with a track record of success: It had been used in religion a few times prior to the birth of Christianity!

Gautama Buddha – born of a virgin, Maya, 600BC

Dionysus – Greek god born of a virgin in a stable; turned water into wine

Indra – born of a virgin in Tibet around 700BC

Mithra – born of a virgin in a stable on 25 December 600BC; resurrection celebrated at Easter!

There is an interesting comment on the matter in the book *The*

Hiram Key by Robert Lomas and Christopher Knight:

> But for twist of fate in the later years of the Roman Empire, nice families would today be driving to Sunday worship with 'Mithra Loves you' stickers in their car windows!

In her book *Mary Magdalene: Christianity's Hidden Goddess* Lynn Picknett goes on to state:

> Not only does the Nag Hammadi gospel of Thomas state that Jesus had a twin brother, but Mary went on to have more children, presumably by Joseph, the older man, who was said to have married her whilst she was pregnant with Jesus to hide her shame...

> Also, the Roman Catholic Church idea that Mary was a virgin forever just can't be true. It is no secret that Mary went on to have more children: 'Is that not the carpenter's son? Is not his mother called Mary? *And his brethren, James and Joses, and Simon, and Judas?* (Matthew 13:55)

Jesus born of Mary, whose father some incorrectly assume was a Roman centurion, was the stepson of Joseph and later he had four stepbrothers. But Jesus was indeed different.

The birth of Jesus is covered in the Bible in varying ways. Matthew 2:1 states quite clearly that Jesus lay within a house: 'And when they were come into the house, they saw the young child with Mary his mother, and fell down and worshipped him.' Matthew says Mary was a virgin but Mark does not. We now know that virgin is a misinterpretation of the word *Almah* meaning young woman. This alone throws into disarray the incorrect 'Virgin birth' teaching of the Church. Luke is the only gospel that mentions a manger and no gospel mentions a stable.

So Jesus was born into what was essentially an Egyptian family. Following Herod's wrath after the census, they fled back to Egypt.

There is an astonishing gap in the biblical account of Jesus' life from that time until his 16th birthday. He grew up mostly in Qumran. He learned the healing of the Essenes and the ways of Gnosis, itself linked to higher spirituality. By the time Jesus was in his 20s he was already surpassing his elders both in healing and his spirituality. Jesus' felt that his spirituality had reached its zenith at Qumran, and with his parents' blessing he travelled back to Egypt, for he was driven to seek out the astronomer priests of Heliopolis. He had to meet them and learn more about 'The Way', the basis of the priests' teachings.

It was just before Jesus left Qumran that Joseph and Mary sat Jesus down and told him of the events that had led up to his birth. Jesus had always known that Joseph was not his real father but to Jesus he was a superb father and a wonderful man who had taught him much.

Joseph told Jesus that during Mary's pregnancy with Jesus he had told her who her strange companion was, for Joseph also knew him and had watched as he got closer to Mary. He told Jesus that the time was right for him to seek out the priests. Jesus asked more about his real father but Joseph only referred him to the priests. 'They will enlighten you more,' he said.

Jesus became determined to seek out the priests. He hoped above hope that the priests would give him an audience because of his deep connection to spirit and his sheer determination! The priests, however, were notoriously secretive and were rarely seen. The knowledge they held was millennia old and the Essene elders told of fascinating laws of the cosmos and of the building of the Pyramids and races of people long gone. Jesus' deep involvement with spiritual matters was what urged him, almost pushed him, on. Whenever in prayer he asked, 'What shall I do?' The answer always came: *Egypt, priests.*

And so the time came to offer his fond farewells to his father and mother and start his long journey to the Heliopolis astronomer priests in Alexandria in northern Egypt. His parents, as well as those close to him, knew that this man was special. A deep feeling of love and peace enveloped all those who stood near him. He loved everyone and everything in nature so very much. Here really was a very special man. A man in whose company many just stood in awe, listened and were amazed. But something drove Jesus on. Something deep inside him told him that there was so much more to learn, and so much more that he had to do.

Jesus' journey was long and arduous but he was on a real quest. Only with the astronomer priests would he find the answers to the real meaning of life. Driven on and on by some invisible spiritual force within him.

His long journey took him up the Nile path to the island of Philae where he saw a temple with an inscription over the entrance that read 'Come to me all you who are burdened and I will set you free'. The words inspired Jesus to enter this, the Temple of Isis. Those words would later be used by Jesus in his teachings.

Jesus met many of the initiates of the temple and stayed there with them for many weeks, becoming an initiate himself. Among others, he studied the Egyptian Book of the Dead and this too influenced his teachings. 'My father's house has many mansions' is taken from it. The Lord's Prayer, that he was to use later, is in fact the Isis Prayer. It contains 'Amun Amun who art in heaven' and 'On Earth as it is in heaven' or 'as above, so below' which we will come back to later.

Jesus felt at home in the Temple of Isis and it was here that he met a certain high priestess with who he was very impressed, both with her deep spirituality and her striking beauty. They spent many hours together deep in spirit. The hours turned to days and the days to weeks. The name of the high priestess was Mary Magdalene.

Mary Magdalene is the name of the woman that the so-called Christian Church has defamed mercilessly, relentlessly and unflinchingly. They have defamed her character and her memory for 2,000 years. The lies go on. But Mary was not a whore. Mary was not a prostitute who 'perfumed herself with forbidden acts'. On the contrary, Mary too was a great spiritual being.

Her background is at best sketchy and not easy to piece together. She was Egyptian/Ethiopian in origin and sister to Martha and Lazarus (Simon Zealotes). Her skin was dusky, as was John's and Jesus' for they too were Egyptian. It is highly likely that

John and Mary knew each other well, working as they did in Egyptian temples dedicated to the Heliopolan truth.

The Egyptians addressed their Queen Isis as Mistress of the Gods – Thou Lady of Red Apparel – Mistress and Lady of the Tomb. Traditionally Mary Magdalene has been depicted wearing a red dress due to her high ranking in the Egyptian temple of Isis. However, the rather ignorant and very male-dominated Christian faith has completely misinterpreted this for its own ends, describing her as a 'scarlet woman'. We will later see that it was Mary Magdalene who presided over the healing and the rituals in Jesus' 'tomb'. Understanding all this makes what has been lost or altered fall dramatically back into place.

Mary told Jesus of her family, of Martha and Lazarus (Simon Zealotes). It is a scenario one can only imagine with reverence and humility. A high priestess in the Temple of Isis and a deeply spiritual and divinely ordained teacher and healer discussing the world and what the true meaning of life really is, surrounded by an aura of all-consuming spirituality. They talked of the Romans and their occupation and their cruelty, they talked of teaching the people and of gaining as much information and wisdom as possible from the priests from Heliopolis.

On a daily basis many people came to the temple to pray. People came who were sick and Mary watched as Jesus healed so many of them with his knowledge. Some of them he told to go home and they would start to feel better, then Jesus called upon the angels to heal those people – and they did.

After a long time healing and teaching at the temple Jesus felt compelled to go on as a matter of urgency. It was as if every fibre of his being was pushing him on. He knew that he had to travel north to Alexandria and to the astronomer priests.

But something else had been happening at that temple on the Nile, something that Jesus had not imagined in his wildest dreams. He and Mary had grown very, very close. It was clear to those around that the two were very much in love. They were so very close both in what they believed and their way of life, it was a natural progression for them to be together.

The day before he was due to leave Mary explained that with the fall of Heliopolis 200 years before much had been lost. Now most of the knowledge was contained on parchment or papyrus that the priests guarded with no fear of death. She explained that originally everything had been copied twice but that one copy of 'The Way' had been entrusted to Moses. He was to impart the knowledge contained therein to his people on Mount Herob in Sinai. Unfortunately Moses was angry at what met his eyes when he returned to them and he had literally 'laid down the law'. He gave them the rules and only the rules taken from the Egyptian Book of the Dead.

Mary went on to say that Moses had been an Egyptian. He also knew the priests at Heliopolis and their teachings. That is why, when he needed to inspire his people on Mount Herob in Sinai, he did not go to the mountain and receive the word of an angry God on tablets of stone. Moses journeyed back to Heliopolis, was given a copy of The Way by the priests and took passages from the Egyptian Book of the Dead, namely:

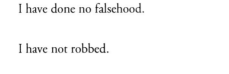

I have done no falsehood.

I have not robbed.

I have not killed men.

I have not committed perjury.

I have not sexually misconducted myself.

I have done no wrong.

I have done no evil.

I have not reviled God.

I am not wealthy except by my own property.

I have not blasphemed God in my city.

Moses knew The Way and this was an attempt to enlighten his people, but he did not inspire them. Moses just told them what they shouldn't do. That was his fundamental mistake.

The spiritual wisdom texts that Moses did not use he preserved, instead of travelling back to Heliopolis to place them back in their rightful home. King Solomon preserved them later in the Ark of the Covenant.

Mary informed Jesus that although the Ark had been hidden on Elphantine Island (close to Philae) following the Persians' destruction of Solomon's Temple, the Ark was empty and the parchments were missing. Jesus was curious. So the Ark, minus the parchments containing the true teachings of wisdom, was on Elphantine?

Mary went on to explain that when the Persians sacked Solomon's Temple they sought anything of value. The guardians of the Ark decided to hide the parchments within the cellar walls of the Temple and surrender the Ark itself if necessary (it being laden with gold and precious jewels). In the event this did not happen and the Ark was rescued. The texts, however, were lost beneath the destroyed temple.

Jesus was all the more determined to visit Alexandria. Mary told him that she had met one of the priests from the church there. He had visited Philae on many occasions and she knew him quite well. He was constantly taking the spiritual teachings to the people of the area and the astronomer priests were pleased with his work. John was his name.

Jesus and Mary were by now very close both spiritually and as a couple and they decided to leave for Alexandria together. They travelled north to the Mediterranean port of Alexandria and to the temple of the astronomer priests. Here, after announcing themselves, they were met by an enthusiastic John.

Let us deal with John 'the Baptist', for far from being just a person who stood in awe of Jesus Christ, and as his precursor, John was a spiritual leader of the ancient astronomer priests' church in Alexandria. In the book *Mary Magdalene, Christianity's Hidden Goddess* Lynn Picknett puts more meat on the bones of this issue. Suffice it to say here that John was a very advanced spiritual being. He taught the Essenes and was a regular visitor to the Temple of Isis.

John was well respected by the astronomer priests. He preached and taught among the people regularly and was enthusiastic about his cause. He ministered and he healed. But he was a quiet and unassuming man. He did not seek to change the world any more than a few at a time. He did not seek to be a messiah. He wanted only to help others improve their spirit and to achieve what they could spiritually during their lifetime. Like a pebble in a pond, he was happy that with every person he taught his divinely spiritual ripples would emanate outwards in ever increasing circles. Loved, revered and well known, John the High Priest taught what he called The Way.

John informed Mary and Jesus that he enjoyed taking the true spiritual message to the people, although it was never to really large gatherings. He said his travels had taken him down to Galilee, where Rome was particularly oppressive.

Mary and Jesus had been at the temple in Alexandria for about an hour talking enthusiastically when a voice called to them from across the courtyard. They stopped talking and all turned to see who was calling to them by name. An old man stood alone and John said quietly, 'He is one of them – an astronomer priest.' It was rare indeed that one of them would appear in public but he called to all three by name and as they walked over it was clear that he was especially pleased to see Jesus and Mary.

'We have waited long for you to come.'

'You are expecting us?' enquired Mary.

'Of course. We have been watching you all the days of your life. We have been longing for this day.'

Jesus and Mary looked at each other with smiles on their faces. Mary moved to help the old priest and all four walked inside.

Down below the Temple of Alexandria they went, through tunnels that seemed to go on forever and looked as though they had been rough-hewn centuries before. They eventually came to a room about 60 feet long and 40 feet wide. It had shelves full of scrolls and books. Two giant tables filled about a third of the room. There sat four old men and two younger ones. Here at last were the astronomer priests who had the knowledge that Jesus sought. The older men were clearly imparting their knowledge to the younger ones, passing a torch to the next generation. But all the talking stopped as John, Jesus and Mary entered. Then, just as suddenly as they had stopped, they started again and just looked occasionally at the trio of strange faces with a certain knowledge of whom they were and why they were there.

The priest who had met them gestured the trio to sit down and almost without another word the other priests gathered round. And then it began.

Mayans, Pharaohs and Orion's Belt

The priests told them that the knowledge with which they had been entrusted was given to man at the dawn of this epoch on Earth, this being the fourth epoch of life on the planet. They explained that this epoch was going badly. The priests went on…

'Over 10,500 years ago the world, our world, was in turmoil. The calendar for the third epoch had concluded, ending with a cataclysmic rising of sea levels that engulfed huge portions of the world's land-masses. Plato wrote of this world event but used the destruction of Thera – the island north of Crete, which he called Atlantis, as the basis for his tale. Plato's date of 9,000 years ago was a reasonably accurate one concerning the event,' said the priest, 'But Thera was destroyed by a volcano only 1500 years ago.' Jesus smiled at the mention of Plato.

The priest, noticing, enquired, 'You know of Plato?'

'Of course,' replied Jesus, 'his wisdom was great. He once said that death was not the worst thing that can happen to men.'

'He was a good student and a very wise one,' said the priest to a surprised trio.

The priest continued the story almost without pause. 'At the nearing of the close of the third epoch of this planet, man had once again fallen into the trap of selfishness. Although his capacity for love and compassion for his fellow humans had grown and evolved with time, so many had suppressed these in favour of greed, manipulation and power.

As in every human culture, at that time there were those who rose above those base instincts and sought a higher wisdom. They knew that such negative impulses and deeds were could only lead to ever-increasing fear and hatred. Ultimately, as the world grew darker in it's negativity, those who wanted to live in a world of love and wisdom retreated to the hills and mountains to live. Theirs was a calmer, more peaceful life - but they were definitely a minority.

Following the cataclysmic event that concluded this third epoch - those small communities, as the waters receded, ventured down to lower ground.'

They began the search to find other survivors - and find them they did. Eventually a group of these spiritually enlightened people found their way to Crete and then further south.'

'At last they found their new home: a land lush and green on the shores of the Mediterranean Sea. Here the people made them welcome. The sages healed the sick with their knowledge of medicine and herbs. They continued in their study of the stars and the planets started by their ancestors and handed down through the generations.

'Of course, Plato was quite correct: the event 10,500 years ago was the dawning of a new epoch on Earth. Although those wise ones who escaped were not aware of it, they were at the very dawning of a new age.

'Time and a few generations passed. Sages died and young sages took their place and in turn died to hand over to another generation. The descendants integrated fully with other people of the land and flourished. The main settlement for them continued to be at the mouth of the great river that flowed majestically into the sea. The river was the Nile. The land was Egypt.

Ten thousand, five hundred years ago Egypt was far from being the scorched land that it is today,' the priest continued. 'Lush and green, it not only enjoyed the flooding of the Nile but it also endured long rainy periods in its warm atmosphere. The land was plentiful, the people were guided by the sages, and all was well.

It was a warm spring day when something happened that would change the world for thousands upon thousands of years. Just before noon something appeared in the sky, high up and slow moving. People working outside noticed it and stopped what they were doing to watch it. Eventually it disappeared over the horizon. Whilst the people were fearful, by the time night had fallen it was no more than a talking point, a topic of conversation, a visit from the gods.

'That night, the sages, the priests of learning, were sleeping when suddenly, in the home of one of them, a child rushed in to its father and woke him. Pulled out of bed by his daughter, the sage went outside. An incredible feeling of peace, calmness and love surrounded him and consumed his very being as he looked at the female standing before him. Young, lovely and serene, she smiled at him. She asked him to assemble all the priests and sages together at noon the next day inside the temple. At that time, she said, they would be given great knowledge of life, the universe and their very reason for being. She smiled again, as if in reassurance, walked into the bushes and disappeared. Never had a man had such a feeling of being in the presence of the divine; such peace and love surrounded her.

'The sages gathered the following day after hearing his story. Some were a little sceptical but all were looking forward to the meeting. When the door finally opened and the visitors entered, all inside were in awe and wonderment. The visitors looked just like ordinary people, and yet it was clear to everyone in the room that they were far from ordinary in the earthly sense.

'They were relaxed and happy as they started to tell the visitors what had happened many years ago as their forefathers struggled against an ever more corrupt and greedy people. They told them how, after much travelling, they had settled in this land, bringing with them the wisdom of love and compassion for all: the things that they had pursued despite the words of others.

'Then the visitors spoke. They told the sages many things. They started by telling them that they should not be alarmed by their presence among them, saying that they had come because it was the beginning of a new epoch for the planet. "The cataclysmic event was inevitable," they said. "When greed, hate and anger take over the hearts of men, displacing love, then eventually they will destroy everything, including themselves. It is a descending spiral into despair as negative emotions control every fibre of your being.

'A new dawn is upon you. Spiritual wisdom, love and compassion travelled with your ancestors away from that island. We watched them sail away, we felt the sadness in their hearts and the grief they felt for their friends who refused to leave with them.

' "We have watched a few generation pass and your love and wisdom grow. Now you are ready, now the dawning of a new epoch is upon you, you must teach everyone.

' "This is what you must teach...

' " You are spiritual beings," the visitor said warmly. "You are born into this earthly existence from the spirit realm, where love and positivity is unconditional and all consuming, where you quite literally exude and become peace and love. You are all sparks, if you will, from the great energy force of light and positive energy that some call God that surges through the universe. You are all part of it and you too are 'energy'. Your body comes from the Earth but your spirit, your soul, the life force energy that makes it work, comes from Great Spirit, the energy force that encompasses and is at the heart of all things: birds, flowers, animals, rainbows, rocks, plants, all are alive in energy."

'There were many questions but the main one was, quite simply, why? Why are spirits born into this life?

' " Imagine if you will – for this is the most simple way that we can put this to you, imagine that the creator, this massive energy force that rules the universe, is light and positive energy itself. This positive force is quite literally love. It creates all, it loves all, it is the epitome of positivity. Each person on Earth is a spark from that light, a spark that strives to get closer to the energy force and become as one with it. To achieve this, the spirit must know love, be able to give love, show love and compassion for everything all of the time, unconditionally, with a free will and a glad heart. Only then is enlightenment complete, the spirit fulfilled. Then all negativity is removed from your spirit and you become as one with the whole.

' "There are nine very distinct levels of spirit. Those in spirit who are at the lowest levels are either beginning the journey or really struggling along it. Then come the levels of elementals, the keepers of Mother Nature's world. Then come the spirits on the Earth Walks. Above them the helpers, then the angels and finally there is the joining. Spirits take on the Earth Walks here or on other planets in other solar systems in order to improve their spirit, to know love, to give it, to become more compassionate, to know the energy force of love within them and to make it grow. For when you show love to a fellow human being or animal, rock or plant, or compassion, or just help them, do you not feel the surge of love welling in your heart? Do you not feel the tears forming in your eyes when you do something wonderful for someone? Well, that, my friends, is your spirit growing in positivity. It is your state of knowing developing.

' "As you live lives and your spiritual development progresses, you will move up through the levels. At the upper levels are the angels. There are angels on some of the middle levels also who come back to live life again, but as they leave childhood they are aware of their divinity and travel in human form to help certain humans. It is the sages, the learned ones, who will recognise them, not fear them, and will listen to them without the cultural dogma of the world clogging their minds. For there are many planets like this one throughout the universe with populations at various stages of social and scientific development."

'One of the sages moved forward.

' "I feel the love and peace that seems to emulate from your very being. Are you these higher beings?"

' "Yes, we come from a world not too far from yours. The stars are countless, the planets surrounding them are more so – there are many planets like this one with human souls. They are at various and different stages of evolution in healing, sciences and spiritual development. Millions of souls on each planet – all are struggling for enlightenment against the materialism of existence on this plane, with varying levels of success.

' "Ours is a planet whose peoples have evolved in to deep spirituality and love. With true knowledge and love comes order and a deep understanding of the cosmos. It comes too with a deep connection to spirit and angels. As we grow closer, knowledge of traversing the galaxy is given to us in order that we might visit and watch over evolving planets. Their distances apart are vast, more vast than you can comprehend. Our planet is orbiting a star that you will later call Osiris; others will regularly visit from a planet that you will later call Digitaria orbiting the star that will later be known as Sirius.

' "Many spirits that are close to the angels opt to live lives as what you may call Higher Evolved Beings. Not always on Planets similar to this one in composition or atmosphere. Therefore some of them look very different both in colour and shape. But all are born of love and light and travel to watch over the evolving ones, you and others like you.

' "We come to you because this is the dawning of a new age. Because civilisation will begin again on Earth and we will give you knowledge that will astound you. We will stay with you here while we teach you the laws of the universe and divine love. You and your descendants will be the holders and keepers of these laws. Teach them to those who seek you, though the populations that are to come will tend to love the treasures of the earthly life more than the quest for enlightenment."

' "How can this be?" asked a sage.

' "There are many worlds that are, as we speak, advanced societies, with scientific advancements that give power, riches and material wealth to some. The remainder of the population strive for this also, largely ignoring their spirituality. There are, of course, those who teach spirituality and many follow, but there are very many who not only deny their spirituality but also laugh at and ridicule those that acknowledge and strive for divinity."

' "That could not happen here," said a sage.

' "Perhaps," was the only reply.

'One of the younger sages offered the comment that if Great Spirit had manifest in some way, then perhaps that epoch may have been saved and all those lives would not have been lost. If you prove to people their spiritual quest with a demonstration of power from spirit then the population will behave!

' "Yes, they will behave, like children chastised for being naughty, being good from then on because they have to. That would hardly be conducive to spiritual enlightenment. The people would not be doing what is right and filling their lives with kindness and love because they really, really want to and need to because they love everyone and feel for everyone – but rather because they had to. Freedom of choice is paramount; divine intervention impossible.

' "Everyone gets little pointers in their daily lives, little clues to the spirituality, a little clairvoyance, premonition, even the sighting of people like us in their craft are pointers to something more than the physical lives people lead. But it is astonishing, the extent to which many spiritual beings on their human journey deny everything but their worldly existence.

' "With a deep love in your heart and kindness and compassion for all of nature, you have a state of knowing growing within you. It is impossible to be this kind of person and not know spirit. It grows within you as your enlightenment grows. Similarly, as your love of the world's wealth grows, or the lack of love in your heart takes over, your 'state of knowing' is diminished. The negative emotions of greed, hatred and anger can so easily grow.

' "You deny spirit, and worse, you ridicule those who embrace it, because in your naivety you believe that your human existence is the extent of all life.

'The sages asked questions and all were answered. Then the visitors left. They did not say where they were staying but promised to return the following day to tell them more.

'On the second day the visitors returned again. The incredible aura of peace and love filled the room once more.

' "Love is divine," one of them started by saying; "love is within all of us, love is in all of nature. The Earth is your mother. She gives you all you need to exist and live well, much as a mother does. The love of a mother knows no bounds and is unconditional. This love, and at this level, is only found in the female. Through the female, a male finds the experience of true divine love, and through making love he connects with Great Spirit at the ultimate level for this earthly plane. Being in love and making love together, you are able to achieve a oneness with Great Spirit that is denied to others who make love but do not progress with their spiritual enlightenment.

' "We see that you have female sages. That is good. Everyone is of equal importance for Great Spirit, for each of you are sparks from the light. But the female you should revere. Only through the female does the male find true and unconditional love. Females, through love, carry new life in their bodies and bring that new life into the world. Their cycle of life and egg producing itself coincides with that of the moon, itself long held as a symbol of femininity and love.

' "Spiritual females should always allow moonlight to fall upon them while they sleep. Females nurture the children, love them, teach them and show them right from wrong. All of this comes from a female living in a world that is far from deeply spiritual, a world that is struggling to comprehend the wisdom that you bring to it. Can you imagine the heights of understanding and love that can be imparted by a female living in deep spirituality?

' "All have much to learn from her. Her chosen male will truly be able to scale the heights of love, pleasure and true wisdom. If he is spiritually enlightened also, they will know true love and achieve a oneness with spirit with their lovemaking.

' "So we say to you today, ensure that the females who are close to spirit are listened to when they speak to the people, for they are wisdom itself. They are naturally closer to love and therefore able to love more freely and unconditionally than the male. It is harder for a male to find his way to spirit and spiritual enlightenment for he has not got the head-start of natural love that the female has. When he achieves it, though, his heart will soar!

' "Now you must record all these things that we tell you for they must be taught to the generations that follow. You should live life in love, respect, compassion and feeling for everyone and everything. You must care for the planet that sustains you and respect all forms of life, however diverse and unlike your own. You must care for all the animals, creatures, trees and plants that share this world with you for they are all your relations in nature.

' "You must also respect the Earth itself, do not mistreat her or damage her. We will show you more of the essences and plants that you will use for healing, remembering that when you take one, you plant another. We know that many of you who are close to spirit use your love and communications with those in spirit and with the angels to heal. You do it with genuine love in your hearts and tears in your eyes; that is why the angels listen and heal with you. Sometimes, though, when a person is not healed and passes to spirit it is because their time here is over. The enlightenment that they wanted to achieve has perhaps happened, or sometimes it is the time that they predetermined to return. You should not feel that you have failed. Your love makes you and keeps you the special spirit that you are.

' "We will teach you of many things over the coming days and weeks. We will show you the movement of the planets in your solar system and the manner in which it affects the people born under differing planetary influences. We know that your forefathers brought some of this knowledge with them, but it is incomplete and we will show you all.

' "We will show you where we come from and we will show you the secrets of medicine, building and architecture, of alchemy and the cosmos. We will instruct you in how to construct great buildings that will stand proud for many thousands of years to come. They will stand as a testament to this time. They will be a mirror image of the position of the stars in the sky at this time. They will point the way to wisdom for millennia to come."

'The visitors stayed for many weeks, though from that point on usually only one or two appeared to the sages on any given day.

'They gradually, and in painstaking detail, demonstrated to them techniques of building and architecture only dreamt of before. They demonstrated the tools for measuring distance, angles and weight. They taught of design with keystones and flying buttresses, the use of huge blocks and gravity-defying lifting techniques utilising the forces of the cosmos. They taught of the movement of the planets around the sun, of the constellations and the true meaning of astrology. They taught of solar activity and how solar flares affect behaviour of peoples on Earth, their moods and their feelings. In alchemy, they taught of using metals for forging, manufacturing and of combining. They taught of flight, of the vastness of space; they reassured them that only the beings who had advanced spiritually to a very high level were ever 'given' the scientific knowledge of the cosmos that would allow them to traverse vast distances to influence others.

'The sages were then instructed to record all of this wisdom on parchments and copper scrolls in order that the generations of sages and wise ones to follow would be the keepers of the knowledge. The visitors emphasised nearly every day that the most important thing to impart to people was that they are spiritual beings on a human journey of enlightenment. That spiritual growth through connection with nature and the love of all people, creatures and things given by 'God' via Mother Nature would lead all men and women closure to spirit and the angels.

They warned that in the future people would become materialistic for the world's wealth and this would harm them spiritually, but that it must not be allowed to get out of control. If the sages and the wise ones throughout the time to come could impart this knowledge with care to a spiritual few then all would be well. And every day they emphasised the importance of the female.

' "Next," said the visitors, "we must construct a sky map, in order that through the countless generations to come, people on Earth will remember this time of communication. This is our first visit of enlightenment for this epoch. The true reasons for this human journey of life must be recorded and held on the Earth in such a way that it cannot be refuted by anyone. There will be facts and tantalising clues but never outright proof. That would remove free will. But for the seekers, those whose eyes and ears were open and had attained a oneness with nature and with spirit, the truth will always be visible."

'The visitors sat by night with the sages, mapping the sky. They stated that on a plateau by the river Nile would stand the monument to this first visit and true wisdom. The sages said that hereafter this time would be referred to as "Zep Tepi" or "The First Time". The Nile, said the visitors, mirrored the Milky Way as it appeared in the sky at this time. They pointed to Orion's Belt and said that they would build, with the sages and the local people, three massive pyramids that would mirror that position beside the Nile, just as Orion's Belt sat beside the Milky Way. This would be done so that future generations could declare "On Earth as it is in heaven" or "As above, so below". They said that the largest pyramid would represent Osiris, which was close to their home. Next they said that a lion of huge proportions would be constructed to face due east, so that the sun would rise between its paws at the spring equinox.

'So precise would the building of the mirror images be that geometry and star alignments would prove to future peoples of the existence of Zep Tepi. "After we have gone," the visitors said, "many temples will be constructed to reflect the knowledge that you have been given."

'Then the visitors gave the sages knowledge of the world's characteristics and land masses, and of shipbuilding and sailing that they said would be employed by the sages in order to traverse the oceans and bring knowledge of spirituality and Zep Tepi to the peoples of the world.

'And so it was that the Pyramids were built and the Sphinx was carved from the solid bedrock. First a gigantic horseshoe was hollowed out, and then rock was excavated from it. This left a large centrepiece which was sculptured into the lion-headed Sphinx.

'The visitors employed superior cutting and measuring devices and techniques that cut off the force of gravity in order to construct the Pyramids with a relatively small workforce of a few hundred people. Blocks of granite that weighed from 16–50 tonnes! Chambers and tunnels linked the great structures underground. The building of the Pyramids incorporated a star shaft that aligned with the only star in the sky that appears never to move due to its polar alignment with the Earth. Much of the lush vegetation around the building area remained intact.

'The chambers inside the Pyramids were constructed to allow access, to those with the knowledge of their construction, to the caverns below. Those chambers and tunnels would hold all the written copies of the Zep Tepi knowledge and teachings including the laws of the cosmos and the spirit world with another copy being held by the sages themselves. The visitors instructed the sages to open a temple of wisdom to give knowledge and wisdom to all those who sought it. They said that the library that they were leaving in the tunnels and chambers under the Great Pyramid would only be discovered if and when all other records had been destroyed and the world had truly lost its way; and only then if a few men and women were wise enough and brave enough and close enough to spirit to seek it.

'Their work was completed. All entrances were sealed for all time. Subtle clues were left behind, like metal doors in the star shafts to name but one. "Those who have eyes to see, let them see," said a visitor quietly as they, the sages, and the building workers stood by and admired the result of their fantastic labours. Amongst that lush vegetation stood three huge Pyramids and a massive lion-headed Sphinx. The Pyramid surfaces shone like mirrors. In the bright sun it was truly awe-inspiring.

'A few days later the sages sat with the visitors enjoying a meal outside by an evening fire. One visitor rose to his feet and declared, "Our work here is almost complete. What we have told you and shown you has been recorded both for your new temple that you will build nearby and for the library that is stored beneath these wonders for future seekers to find. These wonders that we have constructed could not have been built by those on this planet at this time; this will be irrefutable by future generations. We have constructed a sky ground map whereby the Nile river and these Pyramids are a mirror image of the Milky Way and Orion's Belt. But it is a mirror image of what is in the sky at this point only and at no other time. Our sky/ground map will point people of the world towards this time, this date, for millennia to come.

'Even if the wisdom of the sages that we have left behind is lost, this will remain. If true wisdom is lost in the years to come, the people of this planet will come here and stand in awe and wonder who could have built these things, how and why. The positive spirituality that we bring to this place will remain. People will feel drawn to this place, akin to it, as though it were part of them. But the wise ones, the ones who seek wisdom, the ones who retain the divine within them, they will see beyond the awe. For them we leave the proof, for we have constructed these things thus.'

Author's note

I feel it prudent at this point to offer the reader some facts and statistics concerning the pyramids at Giza.

The Great Pyramid is 851 feet high and it is situated at the absolute centre of the world's habitable land-masses.

The four faces of the pyramids face exactly north, south, east and west.

The north facing edge of the Great Pyramid is only three sixtieths of a degree out from true north, the true geographical north and south poles of the planet, not to be confused with magnetic north.

It has been found that these alignments take into account atmospheric refraction. That's the bending of light by the atmosphere and that knowledge had to come from outside of that atmosphere.

The Greenwich Observatory is set to true north and it is 'out' by nine sixtieths of a degree. That, apparently is the best we can achieve thousands of years after the pyramid builders packed up and left.

On the Giza plateau the sun rises 28 degrees south of east on the summer solstice and 28 degrees north of east on the winter solstice. It rises due east on the spring and autumn equinoxes

The Great Pyramid has two shafts running from The King's Chamber to the external walls. One shaft runs north and the other, south. Recently named 'star shafts' they are up to 65 metres long.

The following is an extract from the book Heaven's Mirror by Graham Hancock that offers a little detail on the enigma of the 'star shafts'.

'They were not drilled in when the pyramid was complete but rather they were built in as the pyramid rose in height. Angled shafts were cut through individual blocks prior to being placed into position. The position of the shaft in each block would vary and yet they are placed together with such precision that not even a millimeter gap was ever left. The shafts were then purposely closed at both ends. The shafts align with the North Star, the only star that appears to remain stationary in the sky at all times.'

* * * * *

The astronomer priest continued with the story:

'A few days later the visitors told the sages that they would be going home soon. They told them that they would, however, make many return visits over the ages to come, so that they would always be on Earth for those who seek true wisdom.

'Before the visitors left they instructed the sages to traverse the world for they had given them the maps of land masses and knowledge of where to find the other peoples of the world. "Bring true wisdom to all the peoples," they instructed. And this they did. Via these great sages from pre-dynastic Egypt the peoples of the world were given The Way to spiritual enlightenment. They travelled far and wide across the Earth's oceans, including the land that the visitors called Merica. They travelled to the Mayan, Aztec peoples in South America.'

* * * * *

Author's note:

Whilst you may find the sage's story above a little difficult to believe, the facts are there to bear out what has to be the truth of the matter. As I said at the outset, you must cast off your 21st- century belief that humans are at the top of the evolutionary tree and that we alone occupy this vast universe. I will return to the story a little later but for now we move through time with undeniable proof of the sage's travels to teach the knowledge of Zep Tepi cropping up all over the world.

Inca and Aztec writings refer to the bearded one who traversed the oceans in order to bring wisdom from afar. Despite the terrible and violent history of the Aztecs, their writings tell of a doctrine of non-violence and cosmic gnosis brought to them by a God king called Quetzalcoatl. He had come to Mexico in the remote golden age from a far-off land. He had taught, quite specifically, that living things were not to be harmed and that humans were never to be sacrificed. His teachings were absorbed along with cosmic knowledge and afterlife values.

Native American wisdom, itself closely aligned to ancient Zep Tepi truth, is simply known as The Way.

Also, in 10,500 BC the Mayan temples at Angkor Wat in

Cambodia were constructed using sky/ground correlations. 'As above, so below', or 'On Earth as it is in heaven'.

It is interesting to note here that *The Encyclopaedia of Dates and Events* by L.C. Pascoe cites 10,500BC as a possible date of occupation of America by men who arrived by sea.

The knowledge of Zep Tepi spread across the world. Man produced henges and other outdoor structures to honour the movement of the planets, astrology and the solstices over the ages.

The first wooden totem circle was built at (now) Stonehenge in Wiltshire, England in 9,000BC (approx). In 4,700BC an earthen mound with a megalithic passageway oriented to the winter solstice was constructed in Northern France. In 4,000BC megalithic temples were built on Malta. In 3,000BC henges were built at Thornborough, Yorkshire, England to mirror Orion's Belt and oriented to the solstices. In 2,600BC Stonehenge was built in Wiltshire, England by the Druids. They were visited and deeply influenced by the priests/sages in Heliopolis, Egypt, the site of the sages' permanent home. Stonehenge aligns through the heelstone to the summer solstice sunrise and winter solstice sunset. The Druids were accomplished practitioners of astronomy and astrology.

In 1490BC, during the reign of Thutmosis III, a papyrus gives details of an interesting sighting of 'circles of fire' hovering over Egypt. 'Its body was one rod long and one rod wide, it made no noise.' Later many others appeared in the sky and 'they shone more in the sky than the brightness of the sun'. The pharaoh ordered that what happened be written in the annuls of the 'House of Life' so that 'it be remembered forever'.

Ever since the mystical date of 10,500BC there have been astronomer priests at what has been known as Heliopolis (now disappeared under northern Cairo). The knowledge that they were entrusted with they prized above all else, even life itself. Today, Egyptian texts do indeed refer to that date as Zep Tepi or 'The First Time'. That knowledge was preserved by successive astronomer priests across the millennia. It was entrusted to a chosen few.

Over the passage of time many priests from nearby temples studied with the sages at Heliopolis and later at the Zep Tepi temple in Alexandria, and grew spiritually. Knowledge of personal spiritual enlightenment was always freely given to the people. What was retained by the astronomer priests was the detailed knowledge of the cosmos and the laws of physics, of the planet's land masses, alchemy, architecture, flight, energy, spiritual beings and more that could not be given to the world until sought, upon true enlightenment.

In the book *Mary Magdalene, Christianity's Hidden Goddess* Lynn Picknett states:

> Central to the Heliopolan theology was the story of creation in which the God Atum masturbated himself to an explosive ejaculation, which created the birth of the stars and planets. Long dismissed as primitive – not to say embarrassing – myth, to objective modern eyes it contains more than a hint of intelligent deduction, or even astonishing secret knowledge.

Its system of creation is a remarkable parallel to modern physicist's conception of the creation and evolution of the universe. It literally describes the 'Big Bang' in which all matter explodes from a point of singularity and then expands and unfolds.

In Mali, Africa (in the former French Sudan) live the Dogon people. Robert Temple, in his book *The Sirius Mystery*, explains that their most secret traditions all concern a star to which they give the same name as the tiniest seed known to them. The botanical name of the seed is Digitaria. Temple first came across this strange fact in an account written in 1950 by two eminent anthropologists Marcel Griaule and Germaine Dieterlen of France, who lived with the Dogon and won their confidence. The mystery was contained in one passage:

> The starting point of creation is the star which revolves round Sirius and is actually named the Digitaria star. It is regarded by the Dogon as the smallest and heaviest of all the stars. Its movement on its own axis and around Sirius upholds creation and its orbit determines the calendar.

It is astonishing to scientists and anthropologists today that a relatively primitive people should understand that stars revolve on their axis and follow orbits. It is even more astonishing to them that the Dogon people are correct in that the movement of the Digitarian star is the basis for Egyptian calendar. In his book Temple states that the information that the Dogon possess is easily over 5,000 years old and that they are both culturally and physically descended from the ancient Egyptians. It is not a very big step to assume that the knowledge of Zep Tepi was extended to Egyptian peoples who later descended into the Dogon of today.

It is interesting to note here that Pythagoras, Plato and many other early scholars and thinkers studied with the priests at Heliopolis. Over the millennia there numbered many female priests among them. There was always a woman in the Temple of Thoth holding the title 'Mistress of the House of Books', which included the Egyptian Book of the Dead. (As an aside it is worthy of note that women in ancient Egypt were the freest in the world both legally and morally; a far cry from our so-called Christian Churches whose Bible teaches 'keep your women silent in Church' and who fought the ordination of women, and still do.)

Occasionally in dynastic times the priests of Heliopolis would involve a pharaoh and impart to him the truth and knowledge, believing that through the pharaoh the people would learn The Way. Akhenaten or Amenhotep IV was such a pharaoh. He promoted what we would today call monotheism and it was with he whom Abraham stayed for four years. In the Jewish Bible the first book is Abraham. Abraham teaches monotheism, astrology and the movements of the planets. He teaches of the effect that that movement has upon our lives. This knowledge he received from Amenhotep, who got it from Heliopolis.

The Egyptian queen Hatshepsut also spent time with the priests and promoted monotheism and spirituality. After her death, her son returned to worshipping the sun god Ra and such was her son's wrath that every edifice, statue, cartouche or written record of his mother was erased. Her son was none other than

Thutmosis III, who according to the annuls received a visit from another world.

Ptolomy IV was another pharaoh to find the truth. He ordered the Temple of Maat to be built; on its walls is depicted the weighing of the human heart upon entry into the spirit world.

It is prudent to note here that after the Rameses era Heliopolis, which was established as a great seat of learning, started to decline. The city was largely destroyed by the Persian invasions of Egypt 525–343BC. Miraculously the priests survived as did the teachings and parchments, but they realised the days of Heliopolis were numbered.

They inspired a Church in their ways in Alexandria and their teachings also formed the basis of the Temple of Isis on the island of Philae in Upper Egypt. The work of the astronomer priests had spread further afield also. The Essenes and the Gnostics incorporated much of the knowledge into their teachings. By the first century BC most of the sanctuary and obelisks were removed from Heliopolis to either Rome or Alexandria, now the remaining priests were based at the latter. The remaining structures from the old Heliopolis were used as a quarry for building medieval Cairo. Today all that remains of Heliopolis is a 12th-century BC obelisk dedicated to Sesostris I on the site of the city in northern Cairo.

The Greeks, Summarians and Phonecians all learned from Egypt. Heliopolis was the absolute centre of this learning. At the time of Christ, though, Heliopolis was all but destroyed. The temple at Alexandria and the library contained therein were all that remained. There sat the astronomer priests still, teaching those who came to them. Further up the Nile on the island of Philae was the Temple of Isis; they too taught spirituality on a higher plane.

Although some of the pharaohs embraced the teachings of Zep Tepi, most promoted themselves as the living incarnation of Ra and enjoyed the worldly material wealth associated with such a claim.

Amenhotep IV listened to the priests and inspired Abraham, who spent four years with the pharaoh before starting the Davidic religion of the Jews. Hatshepsut spent many moons with the Mistress of the Books; she too moved towards the truth. Upon her death her stepson removed all record of her and returned to the worship of Ra.

* * * * *

We return to the meeting with the astronomer priests:

'This world,' said the priest, 'resists the truth like no other!'

Jesus and Mary listened as he went on to tell of Moses' visit to the priests and the loss of the papyri without having brought knowledge of The Way to any of his people. The priest told them that the higher-evolved spirits would always be looking after the Earth and were with us always. They lived among us and travelled to and from their planetary home regularly.

The priest then spoke to Jesus, saying, 'I have something to tell you that concerns who you really are.'

Jesus was quiet and he looked at the priest with a slightly puzzled expression.

'Go on,' he said.

'You are son of Joseph and Mary and have been a son to them all of your life. But Jesus…' The old man paused.

'Please tell me,' assured Jesus.

'Joseph is not your real father – this much you know.'

Jesus smiled in acknowledgement.

'Your father was a higher-evolved being, a watcher, as close to an angel on Earth as it is possible to get. Mary knew only that he was a really special kind of man, deeply spiritual, and she fell for him. It should not be hard for you to understand. But realise this, Jesus – he could not stay.'

Jesus smiled again and nodded.

The priest continued, 'He knew Joseph the healer because Joseph had met him a short time before. Your father is a special kind of man, deeply spiritual, and he knew instantly that this man was different. When the time came for him to leave, it was agreed that Joseph would care for Mary in whatever way he could. It was wonderful too that she fell in love with him as the pregnancy continued.'

'Occasionally, Jesus,' continued the priest, 'sons and daughters of higher-evolved beings are born on this Earth. Your birth was planned and foretold. Your mother and stepfather were watched over. The higher-evolved beings guided the maggi to the place of your birth. In the years to come stories will be told of a star that guided people to your birthplace; a star that guided them and stood still above Bethlehem. No star was it.'

Jesus smiled as if the final piece of the jigsaw inside his brain had suddenly been slotted into place.

'Now you know who you really are, you have much to do. Bring the knowledge of life and love that we will give you to the peoples of the planet. Tell them that love is the essence of their being.'

He sat down and looked up at Mary and she held his hand. Jesus now knew for the first time in his life who he really was. Mary Magdalene held him close.

'We waited a long time for you to arrive and you both have work to do.' The old priest then sat down. He looked exhausted and yet elated at the sight of Jesus and Mary together.

Jesus decided that something had to be done to bring knowledge of Zep Tepi to the people; to bring them to understand that we are spiritual beings on a human journey and that 'God' is within us all. He knew that if he was going to have any impact on the world he must be prepared to take on the might of Rome if necessary.

Jesus was also acutely aware of his own ancestry and that he was a Davidic prince. He discussed with Mary the possibility of enacting the old prophecy whereby the Messiah would ride into Jerusalem on the back of a donkey at the feast of the Passover. With this knowledge of The Way, all of the world could be enlightened. There could be peace that would last forever and all peoples would live in harmony. He must fulfil the prophecy. Taking into account his ancestry, he alone was in a unique position to do so.

Mary agreed. John was a little quiet.

The plan was audacious. They would travel back to Jerusalem, for that is where Jesus decided to start his mission. They planned that Jesus would travel the area, preaching and teaching The Way to as many people as possible. At the same time he would heal as many people as came to him who were sick. (And let me be very clear on this point: Much of his healing was accomplished with his training as an Essene healer. He was, after all, one of the most proficient of all the Essenes. But much also came from his deep connection with spirit. For instance, telling the centurion to go home to his wife for she was getting better. The angels themselves allowed Jesus to know this to be so.)

'It is likely that you will have many followers – disciples,' said Mary.

'Good,' said Jesus. 'As many as want to be with me – for we must teach love and compassion as far and wide as possible.'

So here we have the absolute crux of the matter. He was to travel across the land with his disciples and eventually, when he was well known far and wide, he would indeed ride into Jerusalem on a donkey at the feast of the Passover. He would then be declared the Messiah of the old prophecy and 'The Way' would be known to all.

At this time, it is important to know that Jesus had not planned to fulfil the Isis Osiris dying and rising God theme. It did not even enter the minds of the trio. It was totally irrelevant at that time. It would be much later, when things started to go horribly wrong, that the dying and rising God theme would be implemented – but planned to perfection.

John disagreed with the plan at first. He feared for Jesus' life. Mary was sure that this was the course to take and it was as if the angels themselves were influencing them both. Jesus placed his hand on John's shoulder and said, 'The truth must not be allowed to die here.' He looked straight into John's eyes.

John nodded. He knew that Jesus and Mary were right.

And so it was that Jesus embarked upon his mission. He was a real 'man with a plan'. It was as if the angels themselves were with him. He knew that he was doing the right thing. Here at last was his destiny. Now he knew what he had been born to do. All the years of healing and his deep spiritual insights would now be used to benefit everyone. His spiritual connection grew greater by the day. Mary felt it too.

John went down to Galilee in order to help establish a basis for

Jesus to start his mission. Jesus and Mary spent another day or so in quiet contemplation, just enjoying being together.

While John was in Galilee baptising and preaching, some chroniclers believe that Jesus returned to the Essene community at Qumran, others that he went to the desert on a vision quest, much as the Native Americans always have. Jesus wanted to spend time deepening his connection with spirit still further, to give him the spiritual strength to be able to deal with any situation that may arise and offer spiritual answers to any and all questions that may come his way during his mission.

Mary returned to Isis to pray for spiritual help for Jesus in the task that he had set himself. She realised deep down that radical action was necessary for the astronomer priests' isolation was becoming more complete.

When Jesus returned, he and Mary set out together to join John.

John always taught in the open when he was in Judea, thereby denying the temples of their revenue. John's followers in Alexandria and all of Egypt were many and he had quite a flock in Galilee also. The biblical account from here on is inaccurate and the interpretation severely flawed.

John baptised Jesus while Mary looked on. Jesus knew that John was very high in spirit and knowledge of gnosis. Jesus knew that for John to baptise him was right and proper. It was as it should be, for he was baptising Jesus as a practising priest of Zep Tepi.

Jesus went on to recruit his disciples although Mary was always his closest companion and spiritual confidant. The disciples were many more than 12; indeed there were over 70, many of whom were female, *most are totally ignored by the Bible.* The disciples saw Jesus as the Messiah and that was just as he had intended. They marvelled at his teachings and his ability to heal.

The ministry went well. Crowds gathered to hear him speak of love, of veneration of the female, of the wonderful spiritual journey that we are all undertaking on Earth. He taught that the Earth is our mother and that all the animals, rocks, plants, trees etc. are our brothers and sisters in nature. He spoke of 'God' being within us all. He said he would overthrow the Churches: 'You do not need them for God, spirituality, is within us all. Think, talk, spirit listens.'

September AD30: The anointing

This is partly covered in the Bible but the significance is not mentioned by the Bible composers or realised by the readers. In fact, the Bible pays scant regard to the event and misses the significance of it totally.

The anointing of Jesus' head and feet by Mary whilst Jesus was seated at a table is an allusion to an ancient rite by which a royal bride prepared her groom's table. To perform the rite with Spikenard was the express privilege of a messianic bride. Only as the full wife of Jesus could Mary have anointed both his head and his feet with the sacred ointment.

The 'miracle' of turning water into wine is not to be taken literally. It refers to the enlightening the people with regard to The Way. In other words, Jesus taught here too. He missed no opportunity. We should also note that Jesus, we are told, *had to* provide the wine at the wedding. According to the tradition at the time, the only person responsible for providing the wine at a wedding was the groom. So Jesus and Magdalene were married and he spoke to all of their guests about The Way. Imagine it: Guests sitting down at this most happy of events, and Jesus talking to everyone about the wonderful gift of life and love.

Peter and Paul, Jesus' closest male disciples, despised Mary. They had a low opinion of women. Many times they questioned her standing and authority. Mary remained in Jesus' shadow during the three years that he taught; always present, constantly assisting both spiritually and as his wife. Always he told her that he would soon fulfil the old prophecy and ride into Jerusalem on a donkey at the feast of the Passover. He would be proclaimed the Messiah and he would proclaim the Church of Alexandria not as a place to go and worship but as a fountain of divine knowledge and healing; not a Church where cardinals and bishops roamed in their finery but a place where you were enlightened, loved and where you found The Way and the truth. Didn't Jesus say, 'I am *the way*, the truth and the life?'

In one of the Gnostic Gospels, The Pistis Sophia, Mary Magdalene is quoted as saying to Jesus, 'Peter makes me hesitate – I am afraid of him because he hates the female race.' And in the Gnostic Gospel of Thomas we find Peter saying, 'Let Mary leave us – for women are not worthy of life.' *It is obvious that Mary is Jesus' second in command here - definately not Peter..*

Betrayal, crucifixion and survival

The entire subject of the crucifixion is covered brilliantly in the book *The Holy Blood and the Holy Grail*. The authors, Michael Baigent, Richard Leigh and Henry Lincoln, argue convincingly using historical evidence that although 'handed over' Jesus was actually taken down from the cross before death and healed by his Essene friends. Jesus was carried away from the scene by his brother James (Joseph of Arimathea) and taken to his private garden for healing.

But how did Jesus' mission go so horribly wrong? Well, first he confronted head-on the members of the Sanhedrin, and added to this is the fact that the Pharisees despised him and his teachings for they threw into question their very structure. He made enemies, very powerful enemies, themselves blinded to the spiritual truth by the fruits of their very lucrative existence. To believe in him was to deny what they stood for, not to mention their positions of power.

There was a time, shortly before the famous Last Supper, when Jesus and Mary knew that it had all gone wrong. They reluctantly came to the conclusion that Jesus would have to appear to make the ultimate sacrifice and thereby add incredible weight to his position with the populace as the Messiah by bringing into play the dying and rising God scenario. The story of a dying and rising God was not new, not even at that time. At the heart of the Isis cult also was the story of the dying and rising God Osiris and his Goddess Isis. If Jesus was to take on the role of Osiris, *then Mary would take on the role of Isis.* This is an important point to remember.

Jesus and Mary knew the risks. They knew that he might be crucified: tied to a cross, taunted and left to die. There were very grave risks, but it was all about ensuring that his brother James was there with the Essenes. It was crucial that he be taken down from the cross long before death. Mary was distraught but had enormous confidence that he could see it through and that he would live. Mary was at this time pregnant with their first child. Heaven alone knows what must have been going through that poor woman's mind. Nobody could have known or foreseen that Jesus would be secured to the cross with nails through his hands and feet. Nobody could have known the untold agony that he would have to endure, if indeed he could endure it. Could it possibly get any worse?

Very quickly Jesus had to meet with the closest of his friends, the Essenes, as well as with Judas and James (Jesus' brother – also known as Joseph of Arimathia.) The Essenes would administer a drug to Jesus whilst on the cross. It would simulate apparent death and should convince the guards to surrender the body. It was risky and once administered they would not have too long to administer the cure. Time was of the essence.

And so the plan was born. Jesus would be handed over to the Sanhedrin, and he gave Judas the task of doing just that.

Now the Sanhedrin never usually met at the Passover but it did not take a lot to get them to call a hasty meeting. After all, this man was a troublemaker and here was an opportunity to be rid of him once and for all.

When the Last Supper neared its end, Jesus leaned over to Judas and said quietly, 'Do it now.' Judas was far from the traitor who betrayed Jesus. His part in the plan was crucial.

Contrary to the Bible story, Jesus did not have a very public execution. He was, in fact, crucified in a small area near some land owned by Joseph of Arimathea. Nearby was a private garden containing a tomb-like structure. Watching close by were Jesus' Essene friends, frantic with worry about the barbaric wounds inflicted upon his wrists and feet. Whilst on the cross Jesus was administered a herb on a sponge that caused him to lose consciousness.

Joseph then managed to convince the Roman guards that Jesus was dead and they surrendered the 'body' to him. Not an easy task removing Jesus from the cross, but it had to be done quickly. Joseph and the others took Jesus to the 'tomb' where his friends, the Essenes, feverishly worked on the apparently lifeless body. They tended the massive wounds on his wrists and feet, as well as the wounds on his back from the lashings he had received. It took all of their knowledge and dedication. They tended his spiritual needs also. No one expected Jesus to suffer on the cross the way that he had: the lashings that he and only he received, the brutal nailing of his hands and feet. Like the Catholic Inquisitors that were to follow them, the Sanhedrin revenge was total. Jesus was in a much worse physical state than his friends ever expected to see. But his spiritual and physical determination was unbelievably strong.

Mary went to a quiet area of the desert terrain on her own, very private vision quest. She asked for only one thing: that her man should survive, for they still had much to do. She got the answer she needed to hear and returned to be with him. Once back at the tomb Mary cared for Jesus and assisted the Essenes during the next couple of days. On the third morning Jesus had recovered sufficiently to be walking around, albeit slowly. His wounds were healing well.

After a slightly better night's sleep, Mary walked close to the garden that morning and was met by an Essene healer dressed as always in white. She looked to a nearby cemetery. The healer smiled, looked at Mary and said the line now accredited to an angel: 'Why look for the living among the dead?' He went on to say, 'Go to him; he is anxious to see you.'

Mary was at the crucifixion and was with him throughout the healing. It is she whom Jesus asked to take the news of the 'resurrection' to the other disciples. The very early Church recognised her true place when they gave her the title 'Apostola Apostolorum' – Apostle of the Apostles or The First Apostle. She was known even at that time to be second only to Jesus – *not Peter*. If only the people of that time had known that Mary was at least Jesus' spiritual equal.

As mentioned in *The Templar Revelation*, the question must be asked: Where were all the male disciples? They certainly weren't at the crucifixion; only Mary Magdalene, Jesus' mother Mary and Martha are mentioned. The male disciples fled after the last supper and kept their heads low! They *all* deserted him. So much for the male-dominated Church that has no time for women as leaders. They listen too much to the words of Paul and Peter. It does them no credit. Does not one person in the Christian Church realise that it was the females who stood by Jesus through the crucifixion and beyond – long after the men like Peter had not only fled the scene but also repeatedly denied him? Is this the man to whom the pope of the Roman Catholic Church is ordained to be a successor? Irony indeed. Actually it may be rather fitting that the corrupt and manipulative Church of Rome allies itself so closely to one who ran away, denying all knowledge of Jesus.

After the so-called resurrection Jesus was still weak and in a certain amount of pain from his ordeal, but he and Mary met with the Essenes and Joseph. Joseph told them that it was too dangerous for Jesus there now and perhaps he should lie low for a while. And in any event, a rising God does not stay around! Jesus went to meet his disciples and they were upset that he had met Mary first. Peter's hatred of women grew. Jesus told them to carry on teaching The Way, although he doubted that Peter had really grasped his teaching considering his dislike of women in general.

Jesus and Mary decided to travel in separate directions temporarily. He knew that his high profile days were over and that from now on he was going to carry on teaching, but now more like John had always done. His thoughts concentrated now on his wife and his future role as a father. He hoped that his disciples, those Nazarenes, would continue his work in their area. He hoped that his work would not be in vain. There was still Alexandria, there were still the disciples and he knew that the Essenes and others would document what had happened and what he taught. With a dying and rising God at its head, the truth about The Way and Zep Tepi was assured, surely?

Jesus told Mary that she should go with her family to Gaul. It would be a new start in a thriving and lush green area. He told her that he would join them soon. And so it was that Joseph, Mary, Martha and Lazarus travelled across the Mediterranean and landed in Marseilles. Jesus did indeed join them later. He wanted to spend just a little longer around Jerusalem, albeit incognito.

After Mary Magdalene settled in France in the area known as the Languedoc, she gave birth to her daughter Tamar. Despite Jesus' frequent travels to such places as India and Ethiopia, preaching spiritual enlightenment, he also spent as much time as possible in France with Mary and Tamar. They had two more children during the next few years, Jesus Justus and Joseph.

It was during one of his times away that Jesus encountered Saul on the road to Damascus. Jesus was angry that Saul had turned his back on him in favour of Rome. It was after this chance meeting that Saul became Paul, saying that he had seen the resurrected Christ. And so it was that Jesus and Mary's dying and rising God scenario received recognition and took hold. Paul preached the resurrection but embellished it to demand subservience through guilt. The 'fact' that the risen Jesus had 'appeared' to him he used to his advantage in his doctrine. Far from teaching The Way, Paul used this meeting to his own advantage.

And that was the start of control of the people and the beginnings of the Church of Rome. It was also the act that sealed the fate of millions of people to life in the spiritual wilderness for the next 2,000 years. The Way and the truth came into the world. But it was buried by the Church.

Spirituality crushed, and the controlling Church is born

In France the spiritual enlightenment that Mary and the others taught spread across the region like a breath of fresh air, the doctrine of true divine love and compassion touching a chord with the people. Jesus' brother James travelled to England and was granted 12 hides of land at Glastonbury. He was visited later by Mary with her daughter Tamar. It is said that the river Tamar in Cornwall is named after her. Meanwhile in the Languedoc Mary Magdalene's teachings went on and the Zep Tepi way of living took a firm hold.

In AD49 Joseph of Arimathea visited Glastonbury with Jesus Justus, eldest son of Jesus and Mary Magdalene. It was now a thriving community. Jesus Justus dedicated a stone in a new chapel to his mother Mary. It is still there today. *It is not, as the Church will tell you, dedicated by Jesus Christ to his mother the 'Virgin' Mary.*

In AD63 Mary died at St Baume and was buried at St Maximus in Provence.

There are many theories as to the eventual end of Jesus of Nazareth and scholars argue over the evidence of various chroniclers. At the end of his life it is said that Jesus Christ joined the fight against the Romans and, according to some chroniclers, died at the siege of Masada. Others say he died in India and there is a shrine at a site there said to be his final resting place. In the book *The Tomb of God* the authors Richard Andrews and Paul Schellenberger argue that Jesus' tomb is actually in Southern France.

Following their deaths the spiritual enlightenment that Jesus and Mary brought to the world continued to thrive in southern France. Not so in Jerusalem, where Paul had worked on spreading the resurrection story and subservience to the Church through guilt. Paul's zeal in promoting a dying and rising God was very successful.

Against the new Pauline Church of Rome, the Nazarenes offering the true teachings stood no chance at all. They were persecuted, imprisoned and even executed. Dying with them in that part of the world was the spiritual truth for us all. The priests from the Isis temples and the temples of Alexandria continued to preach the truth but were completely overshadowed by the zeal of the new Church of Rome with its promises of heaven if you obey their rules and hell if you do not.

Over time splinter groups and differing religious sects were formed who worshipped in different ways with differing dogma. By 300AD what we now term as the Holy Land had Paul's Christianity as the dominant religion but was awash with different sects.

For the next 1,000 years after Mary Magdalene's death the Heliopolan truth and the wisdom of Zep Tepi not only survived but also positively flourished in that small corner of the world that Mary and Jesus had decided to call home. It is as if it were purposefully plucked from the political and religious turmoil of the 'Holy Land' by the angels themselves and granted a safe haven, a sanctuary where wisdom could continue despite the best efforts of greedy and controlling Churches.

The wisdom of the Isis and Magdalene 'cult' was preserved in a society that became ever more spiritually enlightened. The area of the Languedoc shone as an example to the world. They had schools and universities; their wisdom was great indeed. As the centuries crept on a secret few at the head of the society were charged with preserving the writings and wisdom of Mary Magdalene: the writings about Zep Tepi, the Heliopolan truth, her life at the Temple of Isis in Egypt and her life with Jesus both before and after the crucifixion.

The society of guardians was known as the Priory of Sion or Our Lady of Zion – Magdalene.

Author's note

Magdalene or Magdala means place of the dove, place of the tower and temple tower.

In Micah 4:8, a prophecy perhaps: 'And then Oh Tower of the Flock, the stronghold of the daughter of Zion – unto thee shall it come, even the first dominion, the Kingdom shall come to the daughter of Jerusalem.'

In Hebrew the epithet Magdala literally means tower or elevated, great, magnificent.

Mary Magdalene was known throughout the centuries in Languedoc tradition as 'Mistress of the Waters' or 'Mary of the Sea', but the association is always with water. To the Gnostics, as indeed the Celts, females who were afforded religious veneration were always associated with water, lakes, wells and springs. Gnosis (or knowledge) was always connected with the female Holy Spirit – which 'moved on the face of the waters'. This was the Holy Spirit of Sophia (Wisdom) said to be incarnate in Mary Magdalene

* * * * *

Because of Jesus and Mary's re-enactment of the dying and rising God scenario, Magdalene has, since her death, been likened to Isis herself by her followers. Whenever secrecy or coded writings were required, she was always referred to as Isis.

Back in the so-called Holy Land the battle for the hearts and minds of the people raged on. By the time of the fourth century there were many Christian sects, each one differing on how to worship, what Jesus had actually said, what he actually meant and what was and was not considered 'sin'. Though all were originally based on the Pauline doctrine of a resurrected 'son of God' their differences were numerous.

Barbarism of the 'Christians' seals the fate of millions

On 20th May 325AD Emperor Constantine of Rome held the Council of Nicaea in Turkey. Leaders of all the Christian sects were invited to attend the meeting, which Constantine chaired and controlled. The meeting was a stroke of genius on his part. The Roman Empire was beginning to fragment, and Constantine saw the meeting as a way of uniting many of the citizens behind him. Bond all the Christians together in one 'orthodox' religious faith and he would not only be respected by the people but positively revered.

Much was discussed and over the days that followed an agreement was eventually reached not only on the more contentious issues relating to Jesus actually being a God but also what he actually said and what he meant by it. Gospels were chosen, and when their content did not correspond with Constantine's idea for a controlling Church of a dying and rising God, they too were amended. Agreement did not come easy. Sometimes there was so much initial division between the representatives present that the end result was nothing more than a second-rate compromise.

But that did not worry Constantine, so long as all of Jesus' teachings were trimmed to fit this new and emerging Roman Church. Also discussed were the forms of service including when to sit and when to stand. The Church of Rome was born.

All Christian sects united within its ranks. Theirs was the orthodox religion. Anything else was to be immediately branded as heretical.

In 391AD the now unified and therefore stronger Church of Rome and its followers were certain in their doctrine. Rome now gave approval to set into motion the suppression of all so-called heretics by the orthodox Christians. They took extreme measures, persecuting the Isis priests and their followers wherever they found them. Disappearances and savage beatings were commonplace; even death for a heretic was justified and swift.

But as if that was not enough, in an act that was to set the benchmark for ruthless Christians to follow throughout history they destroyed the Temple of the Heliopolan Priests at Alexandria, ruthlessly killing the spiritually wise priests as heretics. They then burned to the ground the Serapeum Library at Alexandria. Rooms, walls, shelves stacked with books, writings and scrolls filled with wisdom from the millennia that preceded these Christians were destroyed in the historical blinking of an eye. That single act of barbarism helped to seal the fate of millions of souls on a human journey for millennia to come.

The Isis cult was suppressed and the Heliopolan truth was destroyed forever by zealous fanatical Christians. But the truth has a habit of surviving and reappearing. Deep under Solomon's Temple certain truths survived, the wisdom of the ancients still had a chance... And under the Pyramids, more!!

In *The Hiram Key* the authors the authors Christopher Knight & Robert Lomas sum up the burning of the library of Alexandria thus:

> The Romanised Church destroyed any evidence that portrayed its 'saviour' as a mortal rather than a God. In one of the greatest acts of vandalism, Christians burned the library at Alexandria in Egypt to the ground because it contained so much evidence about the real Jerusalem Church. In doing so they destroyed the greatest collection of ancient texts the world has ever seen.

So desperate were they that all the truth about Jesus' real life and real doctrine should be erased that they destroyed everything.

In that library, that temple, the home to the Isis and Heliopolan priests, was written evidence of Jesus' visit with Mary Magdalene, his long stay there, his many talks with the priests, his conversations with John the High Priest and evidence of Mary's high priestess status in the Isis 'Way'.

Through the centuries the Church continued its wrongful teaching that the female was inferior and that 'all men are equal' – and only men! Not so the Gnostics, who realised and fervently taught of the importance of the female principle and involved many women in the role of teacher.

When reading Gnostic texts the early Christian Church leader Tertullian was outraged: 'These heretical women – how audacious they are! They have no modesty; they are bold enough to teach, to engage in argument, to enact exorcisms, to undertake cures, and, it may be, even to baptise!'

Tertillian referred to a woman teacher who led a congregation in Africa as 'that viper' His chosen stance was that:

> 'It is not permitted for a woman to speak in church, nor is it permitted for her to teach, nor to baptise, nor to offer the eucharist, nor to claim for herself a share in any masculine function – not to mention any priestly office'

It must be remembered that during his lifetime Jesus talked openly with women, taught with them, prayed with them and healed with them. Even for Jesus this was against the strict Jewish convention. But he did not care about that – he cared about truth and love.

Within two decades of Jesus' death women held positions of authority and leadership in local Christian groups. It is clear that when it comes to a person's spirituality and the ability to impart wisdom, the sexual orientation of the teacher is unimportant. When teaching of love and compassion whether you are male or female is of no consequence.

In the Bible, probably written by Paul or one of his associates, is the following: 'the women should be kept silent in the churches. For they are not permitted to speak, but they should be subordinate… it is shameful for a woman to speak in church.'

By the end of the second century participation in worship by women was expressly condemned. Groups that did not obey this rule were branded heretical.

Yet what did the Church fear so much about women? And how has the rejection of women by the church affected its course over the centuries?

From the very start Peter and Paul were women haters. The Church of Rome, which eventually became accepted as the Christian religion, was devoid of female influence. It truly was and largely still is a male-dominated institution. But if we look at what its guiding principles were and still are then we begin to understand a little more clearly. The aggressive nature with which the new Church of Rome and the emerging Christian religion was formed made 'hard and fast' rules an absolute necessity. The case for subservience through guilt had to be made very forcibly and the men who dominated the religion had to be seen to be in control. Women were considered weak. And with this religion of heaven and hell, God and the devil, and entrenched dogma – there really was no place for the deep, abiding and unconditional love, coupled with compassion, that is found in a woman. Hellfire and Brimstone preachers successfully 'put the fear of God' into the people.

Remember that the Native Americans, when sat in council considering a particularly vexing problem, like the possibility of armed conflict, listened to a woman if she wanted to speak. If one was not present then one or more would be called. For a woman will look at the problem from the point of view of a mother, sister, one who has felt the God-given wonder of life growing inside her, of giving birth and nurturing. She will see also the losses possible on both sides of any conflict. If there is a way around the problem, in all probability a woman will stand a good chance of finding it. The warriors, however, just want victory. Their vision is, by comparison, narrow.

The Knights Templar and the Roman Catholic Church

By the 12th century, 1100AD, there was a spiritually advanced society in southern France in the area known as the Languedoc. Unlike the rest of France, this area stood apart in its deep knowledge of and connection with the spiritual world. The legacy of Mary Magdalene and her husband was profound and marked. The guardians of her writings and scrolls, which they brought with them to France, were the Priory of Zion.

The Romanised Church had, by now, grown beyond recognition to be known as the Roman Catholic Church. Its doctrine of subservience through guilt and the story of the dying and rising God born of a virgin were accepted throughout the world as fact. It jealously and ruthlessly guarded its position as the dominant religion on Earth and its corruption continued unabated.

Worried at the rise in power of the Roman Catholic Church, the Priory of Zion, under the leadership of Hugh de Payens, met at his home in the Aude Valley in the Languedoc, just a short distance from the village of Renne le Château. Magdalene's writings and that of her descendants continually referred to the Zep Tepi scrolls that remained lost in the catacombs of Solomon's Temple. Hugh de Payens put forward the case for retrieving them to the assembled members, stating that they were the original contents of the Ark of the Covenant. 'The Priory,' he said, 'must ensure that these scrolls, if they are still in existence, are returned to France for safe keeping. They are all original writings and we must not let them fall into the hands of the corrupt Roman Catholic Church.'

They eventually agreed to form a new group, which would consist of a group of knights who would seek permission to go to Jerusalem, ostensibly to guard the streets and keep the people safe from Saracen attack. They would seek permission to be stationed at the temple site, the Dome of the Rock, as this would make their search a little more discreet. And so the Knights Templar were born. As the Knights Templar, Priory members could act without arousing suspicion from the Church.

The Poor Knights of Christ duly received their permissions and in 1119AD nine Knights Templar set out for Jerusalem headed by Hugh de Payens himself. Welcomed by the authorities as protectors, the Knights Templar were afforded every privilege and comfort and were, in accordance with their wishes, stationed at the temple site. Whilst one or two of them patrolled the roads around the city the others searched the catacombs and underground areas for the scrolls.

After excavating extensively they eventually made a startling discovery. Indecipherable scrolls were unearthed from an alcove in a lower wall. De Payens knew he had the Zep Tepi scrolls from the Ark of the Covenant. Imagine it: He had in his hands the very scrolls that Moses himself had borrowed from the Heliopolan priests.

De Payens and one other of the knights returned almost

immediately to France with their most treasured of possessions wrapped in cloth for the journey. What Moses had originally borrowed from the Zep Tepi priests was not only the essence of the Egyptian Book of the Dead but also much of the wisdom from the visitors' time with the original sages. The scrolls contained all the knowledge of alchemy, architecture and sciences of the cosmos. They were a true find!

Once back in France at the home of Hugh de Payens the Knights Templar concealed the scrolls once again. They then agreed that as the power of the Church of Rome grew it would be a good idea to increase the order of the Knights Templar; their own army of protection for the Zep Tepi truth: knights capable of protecting the Priory guardians and the secrets of Magdalene and John the Baptist, both Isis and Zep Tepi high priests. (To them Jesus was secondary. It was Mary and John who were the closest to Zep Tepi. Jesus was the person who came along later. It is interesting to note here that to outsiders the Knights Templar were known as the Poor Knights of Christ, but were also known as the Order of Saint John [the Baptist].)

Over the coming years the Templars did indeed grow in number and in influence too. They were accepted by royalty and, believe it or not, the pope! The Templars used building skills gleaned from the scrolls to design and build Chartres Cathedral in Paris. It was magnificent with flying buttresses and the sheer scale of the north tower typified coming Templar designs. They left many clues in Chartres, still there today 'for those who have eyes to see'. It is clear that they carried on the work of the original sages and visitors in subtle clues left behind for the initiate. There is a depiction of the Ark leaving with Sheba for

Ethiopia. This section of the Cathedral is known to this day as the 'Doorway to the Initiates'. The building of such a Cathedral here at Chartres was no hit-and-miss affair on behalf of the Templars. It was meticulously planned and executed. The site was selected because it was the site of an original temple to the Goddess Isis. It sits squarely on the Paris meridian. It is adorned with numerous statues of Mary Magdalene, likening her to Isis herself 'for those who have eyes to see'. The city of Paris itself was named after the original temple that stood here: Per Isis = Paris.

The Catholic occupation of the cathedral has not been without incident. In the 1500s a woman claiming to be a priestess of Isis stormed into the cathedral and demanded the return of a carved wooden statue once housed in the original temple. She informed the Catholic priests that the alter itself contained imagery of Isis and Osiris. The priests acted swiftly. They had the alter and statue smashed and burnt. They declared the woman a heretic and promptly tortured and burnt her too!

Templars' (and later Freemasons') decorations in some of the Templar built churches are clearly astrological by design. These decorations reflect the old adage of the initiates: 'As above, so below.' This is a clear reference to the sky/ground correlations between the Pyramids and the night sky at the time of Zep Tepi. Deep in Chartres Cathedral there is a carving depicting Mary Magdalene with the Ark, further proof of Templar knowledge of Mary and Zep Tepi.

The pope's bloody genocide in the Languedoc

The Church of Rome, becoming increasingly worried at the meteoric rise in stature and influence of the Knights Templar, acted quickly. Pope Innocent II bestowed on them many favours, privileges and lands. He then issued a papal bull stating that the Knights Templar were answerable to no man, king or queen, no power on Earth, save the pope and the Church of Rome. It was a dangerous marriage for the Priory, having the Church so closely involved with the Knights. Perhaps they thought, even at that time in history, 'Keep your friends close – and your enemies even closer!'

As guardians of the Magdalene legacy, the Priory of Zion were able to remain in the shadows over the years as the Knights Templar were in the public eye continually. Only a very few leading Templars were aware that the Priory were the real leaders. But fate was about to take another terrible turn.

The Magdalene legacy in the Languedoc did not go unnoticed in Rome. 'This heresy should be erased from the face of the Earth,' declared the rather ironically named Pope Innocent III. This advanced society posed a very real threat to the Church of Rome. The pope continually heard of their teachings and the claim that theirs was the truth and The Way. Now the Catholic Church was about to set out on a mission of genocide on a horrendous scale in the name of Jesus Christ. A frightened and corrupt Church set about destroying the Magdalene truth once and for all.

In 1209AD Pope Innocent III launched the now infamous Albegensian Crusade. It was a crusade of unimaginable terror that was to take an astonishing 40 years to complete. The task for the papal armies was to go to the area of the Languedoc, home of the descendants of Mary Magdalene and the followers of her wisdom (home also to many Knights Templar), and put them all to the sword. Men, women and children, young and old: none were to be spared. Rumours had circulated back to the Vatican that somewhere in the historical records of the area was written evidence that Jesus was alive as late as AD49, and living there with Magdalene and his family. This was a terrible threat to the Church. After all, it would prove that the teaching of Christianity was nothing more than a deliberate lie. Advanced as this society was, it stood for the truth, and the Church of Rome could not tolerate that. The population called themselves Cathars, and the Cathars, declared the pope, had to die – all of them.

As the word spread of the papal armies descending many Templars had already left for the Holy Land and in any event they were not strong enough in number to resist the countless thousands of the pope's bloody army.

Between 1209AD and 1244AD the systematic slaughter of hundreds of thousands of men women and children in the name of a loving God raged on. Mutilations and rape were commonplace. The Papal armies under the command of one Simon de Montfort executed their terrible deeds year after

127

bloody year. There are places today in that part of France where his name still invokes shudders down the spine. Whatever the religious reasons for this genocide they soon became mixed with political ones. The area that was the Languedoc with its relative wealth and power soon became too difficult for the armies from the north to ignore. Whatever independence the area enjoyed up until that time was soon extinguished and by the end of the murder spree it, or what remained of it was most definitely part of France

But those invading armies did not have everything their own way. Something quite extraordinary began to occur. In the final years of the crusade many of the soldiers were defecting to the Cathars, despite the fact that they would surely die. Cathars were burnt at the stake in their thousands, yet it is written that they approached their certain death by torture not only with stoicism but also with total calm – even, it is said, when the flames engulfed them. It is recorded that when one Cathar was being dragged away a Roman Catholic priest waved a crucifix at him. 'Take that symbol away from me,' he said, 'it is too young!' What the Cathars were following was, of course, much older – 11,000 years older!

The rivers of the Languedoc ran red with the blood of the spiritually enlightened. The smoke from the burning of the innocent blackened the sky year after bloody year. For 40 years the agonised screams of the tortured filled the air. Then, finally, the Languedoc fell silent, the armies retreated north and a vast swathe of southern France fell into darkness indeed. The Roman Catholic Church had done its worst. In Rome the pope and his cardinals walked the corridors of the Vatican in their fine robes, the blood of a million souls dripping from every fibre.

The Church of Rome had dealt a massive blow to spirituality. They had struck at the very heart of the teachings of the angels themselves and of the advanced beings that have been among us since Zep Tepi. Their arrogance knew no bounds. If any bloodline of Jesus Christ and Mary Magdalene had still existed in the Languedoc, they had surely succeeded in snuffing it out.

Be sure of this: The Church of Rome is not all about love and it never was. It was then and still is to this day all about control and power. They deny the truth and the true work of the angels themselves, folly indeed.

The Priory of Zion, though, survived. The Zep Tepi scrolls survived, in the old home of Hugh de Payens, a safe Templar haven, across the valley from the small Roman Catholic Church of Renne le Château.

After a dark 60 years in southern France with spirituality all but extinguished, Catholic priests finally ventured into the Languedoc to take orthodoxy to a slowly repopulating area. They had their informers, though, who freely gave away the names of leading Templars who were, in turn, protectors of the Priory. And whilst the Priory was shadowy and unseen and therefore it was not easy for the Church to pinpoint individuals, the Templars, on the other hand, were an open book.

Friday 13th for the Templars

In 1307AD King Phillip the Fair of France, uneasy at the power and influence of the Knights Templar, requested an audience with the pope. As far as he was aware the Knights were controlled by the Church (due to the papal bull issued years before) and he was therefore unsure what the outcome of his meeting would be. He was surprised to learn that the pope too was concerned about the Knights Templar. The pope's concern centred on their integration with the Priory of Zion, but he kept this a secret from the king.

The pope pretended to share the king's concern regarding the rising power of the Knights, and so it was that in that year came the Knights Templars' spectacular fall from grace. Secret orders were issued to the king's aristocratic representatives and the Templars were rounded up on Friday 13th October 1307, arrested, tortured and burned.

But that was far from the end of the Templars. They were spread far and wide and the truth is that relatively few were actually executed. Their grand master though, one Jacque de Molay, was eventually slowly roasted to death in the shadow of Notre Dame Cathedral. First his inquisitors placed a crown of thorns upon his head and taunting and wounding him. After the roasting his lifeless body was wrapped in a cloth. Some say that this cloth is the Turin shroud. Carbon dating has recently refuted the idea that it could have been the shroud of Jesus – but it is more than possible that the image contained therein could be that of Jacque de Molay. Of the thousands of others, only those who refused to confess to all manner of heresy were killed. Many Templars, in order to escape the wrath of the Church, fled to Scotland where Robert the Bruce did not recognise papal orders. Here was a haven for the persecuted Templars.

Today just outside Edinburgh by a small village called Temple stands Rosslyn Chapel. This 15th-century Templar-built chapel is in fact a reconstruction based on the plan of Solomon's Temple and the imagery of the Nazarene description of a new Jerusalem. It is covered in Templar, Masonic and Celtic carvings but has *no* Christian imagery. It has carvings and sculptures of Aloe and Maize – plants not found anywhere in the known world at that time, but common to the continent we now know as America.

When the Templars fled the wrath of the French king and a pope they had served so well, they fled to both the USA, as it is now known, and Scotland. *The Hiram Key by Christopher Knight & Robert Lomas* takes up the story:

> We cannot be sure from the surviving evidence but stories persist of Templar ships going to Scotland and to Portugal. The fleet could have visited both refuges in turn, but it seems more probable to us that they divided as soon as they left port, with one section heading for Scotland, and the remainder sailing to the northern tip of Portugal. From there they set out on a voyage that had often been discussed but,

due to commitments in the Holy Land, had never been undertaken.

The Zep Tepi scrolls told of the land of Merica, to where the original sages had travelled 11,000 years previously, and the Templars in command knew that they had to go there. Whilst some of their ships headed for Scotland and a new life, the others pointed their ships due west. It is now absolutely certain that they landed in the Cape Cod area in early 1308, a full century and a half before Christopher Columbus was even born. Evidence for this persists in Westford Massachusetts in the form of a 14th-century statue of a knight wearing the imagery of the Knights Templar. Other evidence is cited in the book *The Hiram Key*.

But what happened to the original Zep Tepi scrolls? I hear you ask. There are a number of possibilities as to their fate – but safe they are. Waiting. That the Templars were entrusted with their safe keeping at the time of the Albegensian Crusade is without doubt. Word definitely got out about King Phillip and the pope's intentions prior to that fateful morning of Friday 13th October 1307 because it was as the sun rose on that day that the Templar fleet left port with scrolls on board destined for a new and safe home away from the corrupt Roman Catholic Church.

When we take a closer look at the interior of Rosslyn Chapel we see many examples of corn cobs (Indian Maize) and Aloes carved into the block work. These are plants that people at that time should have had no knowledge of and yet they are clearly carved and depicted in fascinating detail. Although these crops were relatively widespread in both North & South America, it is believed that they were unknown to the rest of the world at that time. The carvings inside Rosslyn are not later additions but are carved into the blocks that form the fabric of the building. Therefore the carving must have been made prior to Rosslyn's construction, itself well over 100 years before Columbus sailed the ocean blue!

As an interesting aside we should note that during Cromwell's reformation, the churches around Rosslyn were razed to the ground, yet he left Rosslyn Chapel intact.

Cromwell was a known Freemason.

Renne le Château

Little has really to be added to the story from that time to the present, though there is the interesting story of the 19th-century priest of Renne le Château, the village just across the valley from the home of 12th-century Priory of Zion Grand Master Hugh de Payens. It involves the priest's discovery of certain parchments during the renovation of the church. Upon taking his discovery to higher authority in Paris, he suddenly became accepted by the crème of society as well as royalty! Could he have been noticed by the modern day members of the Priory?

What that priest, named Sauniere, discovered certainly changed his life and he held Christianity in an entirely new light. He built a Tower Magdala next to his church. In Hebrew the epithet *Magdala* literally means tower or elevated, great, magnificent. He renovated the church itself, making it resemble Solomon's Temple. He painted reliefs of Jesus being carried *away* from the tomb at night and there are depictions of the Templars and Masonic rites. He was clearly devoted to Jesus Christ and Mary Magdalene but with vastly different teachings from the orthodox.

On his death bed Sauniere told the priest who had been summoned to administer the last rites all that he had discovered. The priest refused to minister Extreme Unction and left the premises ashen and visibly shaken. The excellent book *Holy*

Blood and the Holy Grail details the story of Sauniere authoritatively and in great detail. But this writer certainly believes that Sauniere found writings detailing Mary Magdalene, Jesus and the Zep Tepi truth. It is more than probable because Renne le Château is in the heart of the Languedoc.

Hugh de Payens' château is visible across the valley from the church. It is highly likely that someone could have hidden the writings on Zep Tepi or the Magdalene cult in the church once the Albegensian Crusade had commenced in all its ferocity. Imagine, the Albegensian Crusade is heading toward the valley, the grand master looks out of the window of the château, wondering where to hide some of the parchments – some of the many writings of Mary and her descendents concerning Zep Tepi – so that they will be safe from the murderous hoards. In the distance his eyes fall upon the church at Renne. What better place to hide them, what safer haven could he find, than a Roman Catholic church?

It is also worthy of note that the Church of Renne le Château was consecrated to Mary Magdalene early in the 12th century – perhaps with influence from de Payens himself?

The legacy

Now here we are in the 21st century and little has changed since then. Christianity, with its dying and rising God and threats of eternal damnation for those who do not obey the dogma of the Church, is followed throughout the world. At the top of the Christian tree is the Roman Catholic Church. This Church has raped, tortured and burned at the stake thousands upon thousands of spirits on a human journey. They were tortured and killed because they were 'heretics', because they dared to hold different opinions than the mighty Roman Catholic Church. Their lust for blood and their sadistic enjoyment of their holy duty in interrogation of 'heretics' should have been sufficient to consign the Roman Catholic Church to the annuls of history as the greatest wrongdoers and most wicked people ever to walk the Earth. The cries of terror from their victims as they endured excruciating agony in the name of a loving God stains the Roman Catholic Church and makes it an institution beyond redemption. It is difficult to believe that this Church still has the power over its followers that it has: power to tell them when to marry and when they cannot; power to tell them that they cannot divorce and they cannot use contraception or abortion. Their strict dogma that has nothing to do with love, compassion and healing is causing misery to millions as they try to live by it.

In April 2005 we learned of the death of Pope John Paul II and then witnessed the creation of the new Pope Benedict XVI. As I watched the lengthy news reports of his selection on TV I was amazed at the comments that were coming forth from the faithful as well as the reporters. Some were disappointed that the new pope has ideas on the dogma of the Church that are so closely aligned with those of John Paul II. What's this? Were they hoping for a pope who would relax the Church rules? As it turned out, yes they were! They were hoping for a relaxing of John Paul's strict rules on homosexuality and contraception, to name but two.

Am I the only person who found this utterly amazing? Is it possible that a new pope could change the view of the Church and relax such strict teachings? The answer, apparently, is yes! And if this did happen, say a less conservative pope had been elected, followed after a few years by an even less conservative pope, is it possible that the coming years would see female Catholic priests, contraception being allowed and even perhaps a more understanding view toward homosexuality?

Now the very fact that a pope can change, or influence change to, the rules or dogma of the Church means they could not possibly be God's rules in the first place, but man's! And where does that leave all the people who have suffered greatly to live by these ridiculous rules all their lives? They struggled with large families because the pope said contraception was a sin. They struggled in hopeless, loveless marriages because the pope said divorce was a sin. Girls who found themselves pregnant were not allowed abortion because that was a sin. The making love was a sin and the girls were treated shabbily in institutions run by nuns who thought the girls were damned anyway, sent there by parents who believed it when the Church told them that their daughters had sinned against God. What soul-destroying controlling piffle. Was it all in vain? Was it all totally unnecessary? If the rules can be changed at the behest of a man then those rules are the rules of men and it follows therefore that they must be completely and utterly irrelevant.

The Earth shift and the dawning of the new age

The truth about your spirituality remains the truth today as it has for all time. The secrets of Magdalene, Jesus and John are guarded still by the Priory of Zion and the Knights Templar. Those other knowledgeable ones, the Freemasons, also privy to the Zep Tepi truth, have lost their way slightly, the master Masons hold the knowledge but at local level the Masons has become more of a 'society of friends' in positions of influence in the community. Many know nothing of true Masonic roots.

So when will the Priory and the Knights Templar show these truths to the world? It is more a question of when the world will be ready to take the truth on board. The world is moving toward the truth a little bit more each day. True spirituality is resurfacing in many ways, like spiritual healing, spiritualist churches, complementary therapies and more.

Jesus said:

> The time is coming when you will hear the noise of battle near at hand and the news of battles far away, for nation will make war upon nation, kingdom upon kingdom. There will be famines and earthquakes in many places: with all these things the birth pangs of a new age will begin.

As the world enters the Age of Aquarius it could just be that dawning of a new age that Jesus was talking about. Certainly we are not short of unrest in the world. And from earthquakes and tornadoes to mudslides and forest fires, our Earth Mother certainly is beginning to let us know that we are harming her.

Consider now the Native American Whirling Rainbow Prophecy which states that as the dawning of the fifth world of peace approaches, the third generation of the white man's children will grow their hair long and speak of love as the healer of the children of the earth. This generation will be seekers, they will wear feathers and beads and paint their faces. It is written that these white-eyed children will be a sign that the red ancestors are returning in white bodies. They will learn to walk the earth mother in balance once more and they will reform the ideas of the white leaders.

I feel that this part of the prophecy has already been fulfilled. The generation of the 'flower children' has passed, the words of love and peace spoken – though largely ignored and even ridiculed at the time. Many of this generation though have stayed on the path and those that have strayed into the world of materialism and greed are re-awakening and remembering once more.

The Whirling Rainbow Prophecy goes on to say that the generation of the flower children will live to see the dawning of the fifth world of peace, and live to see it they have. The prophecy states that as the new age dawns, changes will be felt in the earth mother, in the soil and on the waters and that is certainly true.

As global warming increases and mother nature objects to the ravaging of the planet's resources by the insatiable greed of men, we are experiencing an alarming increase in the number and severity of tornados, earthquakes, floods, landslides, tsunami and the like.

There will be many who carry the wisdom of the ancients, of the sky people, of the red man and of spirit. There will be healers and helpers who will be needed at the time of wars and disaster and they will know all they need to know.

We know that the Mayan calendar draws this, the fourth epoch, to a close in 2012, and no – this does not mean the end of the world, rather a sea change in thinking, attitudes and priorities. It will be a change in people's attitudes toward their spirituality. The truth will emerge and they will see the Church for what it is. They will see true spirituality. At this time the Zep Tepi truth will be shown to all, in order to confirm what is right.

So what is going to happen at the time of the Earth shift? Well, we are at that time right now. The process is underway. It is a process of enlightenment for many, many people and it is growing. It is a shift in consciousness. Just as enlightenment grows, so too does man's greed and his love of all material possessions. The Churches will try to hang on to their old controlling ways and their blind dogma, even in the face of true enlightenment. So in this, the prophecies forewarning the persecution to come for Catholics and other radical Christians are not necessarily incorrect, but perhaps they are misinterpreted by those who cannot see beyond their dogma-blinkered eyes.

The prophets foretell people losing their faith and leaving the Church. Some even tell of the Vatican itself being deserted and the pope fleeing as the Church of Rome finally falls. It is a terrifying prospect for the faithful. I can understand why they are worried. To think of your Church and everything it stands for crumbling into dust with God's own representative on Earth fleeing for his life must be more than a little disconcerting. It would be disconcerting if it were God's representative on Earth who was fleeing! It would be more disconcerting if it were God's Church that crumbled – but it is not.

This so-called Church is a church of corruption. It is a repulsive, detestable abomination and those who walk its corridors of power fear the enlightenment of their flock more than anything else. Their days of control are coming to an end.

To condemn vast swathes of the people because they have 'sinned' in all manner of ways and are therefore not fit to live in 'paradise' will eventually be seen for what it is: one of the Church's fundamental errors. Their attempts to control every aspect of people's lives with the creation of numerous 'sins' against an all-loving God whilst perpetrating murder, torture, rape and all manner of vile undertakings will eventually sound the long overdue death knell for the Church.

As John Hogue says in his book *The Last Pope*:

> The real Last Judgment is the day when judgments as such, not people, are consigned to the eternal flames – along with fear, sin and guilt. In the era of spirituality which is to come, when each person will be known by what he or she feels in

their hearts and the life they live in balance with those feelings and with nature, the labels of catholic, protestant, orthodox or any one of the other 300 religions will be discarded and religion as we have known it will come to an end.

Alongside all of this the wars will rage as man struggles to maintain his material possessions, his lands and his money, and it is Mother Nature who will take them away. Global warming: yes, it is happening and it is all part of this Earth shift. The planet will survive as it progresses towards its next cycle. By the time man has finished fighting his wars the surface of Mother Earth will be scarred and wounded. But survive it will. Churches will fall, financial institutions will fall, the value of money will be redefined and the planet will smolder, and through it all real enlightenment will take hold. If you live a deeply spiritual life then you are already well prepared for what is to come.

Over the coming years the Earth shift will gather momentum. As I have already said, the financial institutions will fall. Mother nature will also become much more restless. Countries will make war on others for global domination. Lies will be told to the people of the world. Those who lust for this power will be under the illusion that no-one is watching. They will be wrong. Unusual and extreme weather coupled with increased rumblings within the earth. Influences in the world will also shift. The yellow and the red will come together. Through all the unrest that is to come a new awakening will gradually envelop people's thinking. After the wars and the civil unrest, global greed will be seen for what it is, for its destructive power will be recognised and this in turn will bring about wide-ranging changes in the culture of everyday life. A more caring attitude will emerge - slowly.

This new caring way of living, which heralds the true dawning of Aquarius, will not be born of anything done by man. It will be the females on the planet who will rise up and say 'enough is enough'. Whether in great numbers or by influence, they will act. They will rise and remove the shackles of religious incarceration and centuries of male rapaciousness. No longer content with the absolute mess that the world finds itself in, we can only hope that women, free of religious intolerance, can become as effective as the females in the Native American culture who sat in council with the men. Remember, they were the ones who were always consulted when a peaceful solution was sought, for she was the bringer and bearer of new life, the nurturer of the child, the closest one to Mother Nature. She was the nearest link to nature herself, present in the council.

Already we see the first ladies of the Arab world blazing a trail for women's rights. These leaders' wives from Jordan, Bahrain, Syria, Egypt and Qatar have already confronted head on issues including sexual slavery, child exploitation, trafficking, prostitution and rape. They have delivered speeches to packed audiences that include politicians, judges and tycoons. As they spoke the front rows of robed and mostly bearded men listened in rapt silence. When they had finished they had not only broken a veil of silence on the human trafficking trade but also had coerced and charmed the assembled crowd into taking action and received a standing ovation. Policies are already changing. Surprised diplomats speaking of the 'phenomenon' of the first ladies who now push ahead with social polices in a way that their autocratic husbands never would.

The dawning of the Age of Aquarius truly is upon us. It is going to be a difficult time. But greed will turn to sharing. Hatred will turn to compassion through understanding. Ravenous economic growth will be replaced by economic contentment. Our quest for more has actually got us much, much less.

George Carlin – comedian of the '70s and '80s – wrote the following piece. It is profoundly true.

> The paradox of our time in history is that we have taller buildings but shorter tempers, wider Freeways , but narrower viewpoints. We spend more, but have less, we buy more, but enjoy less. We have bigger houses and smaller families, more conveniences, but less time. We have more degrees but less sense, more knowledge, but less judgment, more experts, yet more problems, more medicine, but less wellness.
>
> We drink too much, smoke too much, spend too recklessly, laugh too little, drive too fast, get too angry, stay up too late, get up too tired, read too little, watch TV too much, and pray too seldom.
>
> We have multiplied our possessions, but reduced our values. We talk too much, love too seldom, and hate too often.
>
> We've learned how to make a living, but not a life. We've added years to life not life to years. We've been all the way to the moon and back, but have trouble crossing the street to

meet a new neighbour. We conquered outer space but not inner space.

We've done larger things, but not better things.

We've cleaned up the air, but polluted the soul. We've conquered the atom, but not our prejudice. We write more, but learn less. We plan more, but accomplish less.

We've learned to rush, but not to wait. We build more computers to hold more information, to produce more copies than ever, but we communicate less and less.

These are the times of fast foods and slow digestion, big men and small character, steep profits and shallow relationships.. These are the days of two incomes but more divorce, fancier houses, but broken homes. These are days of quick trips, disposable diapers, throwaway morality, one night stands, overweight bodies, and pills that do everything from cheer, to quiet, to kill. It is a time when there is much in the showroom window and nothing in the stockroom. A time when technology can bring a letter to you, and a time when you can choose either to share it, or to just hit delete...

Remember, spend some time with your loved ones, because they are not going to be around forever.

Remember, say a kind word to someone who looks up to you in awe, because that little person soon will grow up and leave your side.

Remember, to give a warm hug to the one next to you, because that is the only treasure you can give with your heart and it doesn't cost a cent.

Remember, to say ' I love you' to your partner and your loved ones, but most of all mean it. A kiss and an embrace will mend hurt when it comes from deep inside of you.

Remember to hold hands and cherish the moment for someday that person will not be there again.

Give time to love, give time to speak! And give time to share the precious thoughts in your mind.

AND ALWAYS REMEMBER:

Life is not measured by the number of breaths we take, but by the moments that take our breath away.

Leonardo da Vinci

Nostradamus predicted that the Church of Rome would fall in 2012. He spoke of Muslim hoards invading Europe, not by invading armies but by integration. Nostradamus, though, we must remember, was a grand master of the Priory of Zion, guardians of the knowledge of Magdalene and Jesus and Zep Tepi, so he had access to the scrolls. Leonardo da Vinci, a man born before his time, they say, due to his knowledge of the principles of flight and his designs of flying machines, was also a grand master of the Priory. That is why he painted tantalising clues to Jesus and Mary's true relationship in works such as 'The Last Supper'. He had to be careful; his works were commissioned by the Church of Rome!

Study the picture of da Vinci's 'The Last Supper'. Just type 'da Vinci Last Supper' into your internet browser search engine. (click on 'images'). It is clear that the figure to Jesus' right is that of a woman. Note the smaller hands. She is obviously Mary Magdalene, Jesus' wife. She is clearly at his right hand and therefore equally clearly is his chosen second in command. All the other disciples to the right of Jesus appear to be straining either to get closer to her or to get her attention. Those on the left are clearly not so keen to have Mary there at all and Mary is clearly shown as leaning away from them. The disciples on the far left appear to be engaging in some kind of a debate concerning her, and almost certainly include Peter, the principle objector to Mary throughout. The three nearest to Jesus' left appear a little less disturbed by her presence and one of them holds a single finger into the air. Whilst viewed as a sign of semi aggression, it is without doubt in my opinion, da Vinci's demonstration that she is 'The One' or Chosen One'. These three resent her presence and the high esteem in which she is held by Jesus. One final observation is that Jesus and Mary appear to be wearing similar clothing both in style and colour. Jesus wears red with a blue cloak whilst Mary wears blue with a red cloak. Whilst da Vinci infers a special link between them, he always implies that they are opposites, a clear message to the observer that they are male and female.

Take a look at another of da Vinci's works – The Mona Lisa – again just type 'da Vinci The Mona Lisa' into your search engine and click on 'images'. What is it about The Mona Lisa that keeps the public and academics alike enthralled. The more you view the painting, the more it appears that this woman, or the artist who painted her, has something to say.

It was not until the mid-19th century that artists really began to appreciate this painting, when they first associated her with their ideas of 'feminine mystique'. Scholars even today marvel at the apparent hidden symbolism contained within.

She appears very reserved, her arms folded, her gaze firmly fixed upon the observer. She embodies a divine mystery. We are drawn to her without really knowing why. National Geographic, in a presentation entitled 'Testing the Mona Lisa' concluded that after rigourous assessment, that she may be pregnant. Health professionals appear to agree, citing the rather enlarged hands, as adding weight to the pregnancy theory.

One critic, Walter Pater said in 1867 that this lady was one who 'had been dead many times and learned the secrets of the grave'. He went on to observe that she was 'older than the rocks among which she sits'.

Since that time the public fascination with the painting has far from rescinded. In fact it has become one of the most famous paintings in the world.

Many have asked the question, 'Who is she?' There have been countless discussions and endless hours of debate on her identity and just why she has been depicted with that wry smile. Many theories have been put forward over the years as to the lady's true identity, all have been wide of the mark.

That all-knowing smile that seems to say 'I know something you don't' is typical of the imagery and irony of da Vinci. This grand master of the Priory of Zion, with his access to and deep knowledge of the Zep Tepi truth, has given us no clues as to who this woman is. Well, at least not in the painting itself.

Unlike 'The Last Supper', where the clues form part of the painting 'for those with eyes to see', the clue da Vinci gives us here is within the title he gave this incredible work of art. She is Mary Magdalene.

Mona is an anagram of the Egyptian God Amun/Amon Ra. *Lisa* is a derivation of L'isa or 'The Isis'. Da Vinci's high priestess of the Temple of Isis was Mary Magdalene.

The Mona Lisa *is* Mary Magdalene.

The smile that says it all and yet gives nothing away. Leonardo – grand master of the Priory of Zion and keeper of the Zep Tepi scrolls – was painting his vision of Mary Magdalene. To da Vinci she was the embodiment of the Goddess Isis and the Feminine Principle.

Is she depicted as almost smiling because her identity is known only to da Vinci? I don't think so. She is painted by him as smiling wryly because the truth that she knew- is safe, very safe.

Knowledge in safe hands is knowledge preserved. She smiles through the centuries of Church lies and corruption. That smile and that name Mona Lisa was lost on da Vinci's sanctimonious Church paymasters. It was his two-fingers to the Roman Catholic Church.

The end of Churches

Now the Zep Tepi scrolls, as well as the writings of Mary Magdalene and the sages across the millennia, are currently housed in safe places awaiting the time when true enlightenment will start to spread across the world, when the people of the planet will once again see that true spirituality comes from within the heart of each and every one of us. They will see that we do not need religion with its various dogma and incessant lies. They will see that each one of us has a direct line to spirit. At that time religion will lose its grip of fear on the people as spiritual enlightenment grows. Knowledge will be brought to us again from 12,500 years ago, the knowledge that Jesus, Mary and John tried in vain to promote. It is knowledge that was hijacked and amended to enable the Church to rule by fear.

When the time does come for the Church of Rome (as well as other religions) to fall, it will fall because the people of the world will know the truth about their own very individual spirituality. It will fall because of its corruption and lies. Jesus, John and Mary all taught that you do not need churches in order to be close to spirit. 'You will not find enlightenment in a church,' they declared. According to the Gospel of Thomas, one of the Qumran scrolls discovered in 1948 which had been hidden during the dark early days of the Church of Rome, Jesus said, 'Do not look for me in churches for I will not be there. Break open a piece of wood, there you will find me. By the rocks and the trees, there you will find me.' In being close to nature you are close to spirit is what he was trying to tell us, and with love in your heart you will find enlightenment.

The Cathars did not use churches; to them the way of spirit was in every thought, every act, every day, just as Mary Magdalene herself had taught so many years before.

The Native Americans led very similar spiritual lives. They did not want churches, even when Christianity was foisted upon them. In their lives, they said, it was important to 'walk the good red road'. Their way of living was to practise what they called The Way. To the ancient Egyptians true spiritual enlightenment was known as The Way. It is more than likely the case that they found the teachings of those sages who had visited Merica 11,000 years before the Templars. Those same sages, one of whom the Aztecs called Quetzalcoatl, must have influenced the Native American way of life. The striking similarities cannot be ignored. In contrast, today's religions and Churches offer unsatisfactory answers to life's questions. Little wonder that many people do not believe in this God of love!

Religions warn of dire times to come. 'The end of the world,' they cry; they warn of Armageddon. Some even proclaim that the end of the world will culminate in the end of the planet itself; that the antichrist will rule for seven years and terror, death and destruction will spread across the face of the Earth. Some religions teach that only their followers will be 'saved' and everyone else consigned to 'hell' forever.

As I have said many times, it is the remit of religion to rule the people by fear: fear of what will happen to them if they don't behave. But the world is not going to end. The planet will not be destroyed. That will not be allowed to happen.

There is, however, going to be what some people refer to as an Earth shift, a shift in perceptions and of consciousness.

True spirituality

'If there is a God why did he/she allow Hitler to commit such atrocities?'

'If there is a God why does he/she allow little children to suffer and die horribly of diseases and conditions?'

'I cannot believe in a God that professes to be a God of love, and allow that to happen.'

Let me try to clarify what is going on here. This planet, like many others, has human beings on it. These human beings are spiritual beings first and foremost. They have chosen to return to life in human form again to undertake this human journey once more. As I have already mentioned, divine intervention is impossible due to the overwhelming consequences for all. This human journey of enlightenment relies upon the free will of the individual. It is up to you whether or not you allow and encourage your spirituality to grow, whether or not you allow negative influences to affect the way you live and think and react and interact. Of course, in order for free will to be effective you must have no proof or conscious first-hand knowledge of the world you left behind or to which you will return.

There is no 'judgement' when you die and pass back to spirit, no heaven and no hell as physical places. When you pass over everyone is greeted in light and love. 'Even the wrongdoers?' Well yes, actually, because we are all wrongdoers. Everyone is living an imperfect life; we all make mistakes. It is just a question of degree.

Those who have done a lot of harm to their spirit or soul during this human journey spend much more time being healed, for they have damaged their spirit, making it impossible to progress further at that time. Depending on just how negative they had been in their lives, it may be that they fall back and have to spend a long time healing the spiritual wounds of that life, so hurt by their own actions do they feel. But all are healed in love and light.

The only hell is the feeling of failure that we endure when we realise that we have not progressed spiritually in life as we had intended, when we realise that we have not coped with life's problems the way we had hoped to when we chose this life. We may then choose to return again to face that problem, in order to hopefully overcome it and grow spiritually. All spirits strive to be closer to 'God', the positive energy force that surges through the universe. The more positive and loving we become towards all of nature, the closer we get. All sparks strive to get closer to the light.

The spirit that was Hitler in that life had to have a tremendous amount of healing before he could return again. But in spirit there were those who needed more healing than Hitler. After all, he gave the orders for the terrible atrocities but it was those spirits who carried out the orders, some with a sense of glee and some with no emotion at all, that were damaged terribly.

Suffer the little children

In this day and age it is no wonder that we ask the questions that we do. It is no real wonder that we curse 'God' the way that we do. We have had 2,000 years of lies, half-truths and ridiculous dogma to contend with. Consequently we only see that to us it is wrong that a life has been cut short and so tragically. We get angry (a negative emotion, which in itself can be harmful to our spirit) and we judge and condemn a God who has got nothing to do with it!

Children who fall ill and die merely return to spirit from whence we *all* come. It is more than likely that the spirit that was the child chose to come back and go through this ordeal and that it was necessary for the further growth of their spirit. The unconditional love that surrounds them and permeates from them during this is indescribable. It will flow to and from all those that surround them. The angels feel the pain, see the pain, and when the time to return is close they comfort the child, nine times out of ten without even the closest of relatives knowing. Many times, though, terminally ill children have spoken of seeing an angel, or Jesus or just lights around them. Part of the process of spiritual development, though, is for the people they leave behind, to know that the spirit of the child is healing, happy and in the company of angels.

Many times though, we do not – we cannot – see the bigger

picture of spirituality and the cosmos because of religion and/or materialism. We question the death of ones so young for we have no knowledge or comprehension of why it had to be – or why the spirit itself chose it.

Our guides work with us to choose a life for us to return to, they guide us from spirit during this lifetime, though we do not always listen! How many times have you ignored that still, small voice in your head, or maybe that feeling that you had, only to find out later that you should have acted upon it? When we pray it is our guides and angels on higher planes who work with us.

Of all the people who come to this writer for spiritual guidance it is the women, the females, who come more often and in greater numbers. The males in our society appear to be more cynical and disbelieving. This is not surprising, though. Males have had 2,000 years of a male-dominated society which has as its spiritual base a male-dominated Church.

Life on other planets

We live in a society that is far from spiritual enlightenment. Anything that has anything to do with natural energies and natural healing is known as 'alternative'! This alone should make us all immediately see that if natural healing and natural energies are alternative then we must be living life in an *un*natural way, and of course we are!

We lead such blinkered, narrow lives. The sum of our existence even now in the 21st century is based upon materialism. Church attendance has never been lower as more people decide that it really cannot be the truth and so live for today. We now have a culture that lives for the fast buck, the next new car, the next promotion and the next holiday. The Church and religion has been responsible for virtually extinguishing spirituality. Subsequently if you were to even mention in public that you believed in ghosts or 'aliens' you would be ridiculed mercilessly. We must all accept, however, that this planet is but one grain of sand on a very large beach and that it is naivety in the extreme to discount life on other planets. It is similarly naive to presuppose that aliens are not both spiritually, and therefore in the laws of the cosmos, more advanced than us. Remember, if religion had not taken over from spirituality, this planet would be much more advanced than it is now.

The spiritually wise ones from planets beyond our minute solar system have been with us since 12,500 years ago. Although they left Egypt to return home, as it were, after their long stay, they have been frequent visitors since. The Nasca lines in Peru are giant markings in the ground that resemble arrows, animals, even a runway. These markings take on no form when viewed from the ground. They only take form when viewed from the air. Are they markers? One significant marking has been known as 'the runway' but resembles a giant elongated pyramid that appears to be pointing 'the way'.

Let us be absolutely certain here. These 'markers' were not drawn by spiritual beings from another world so that they could find their way for the final few hundred miles of a 200-million-light-year journey! The very idea is nonsensical. The markers were put there by races of peoples who knew of the existence of life on other planets, and furthermore, knew that they were frequent visitors.

In constructing these things they were wiser than all the theorists and their dissenters who have argued for and against over them since.

Egypt: the start of it all

Dotted across Egypt are clues to a civilisation that had vast knowledge of the stars and the planets. They built temples using 200-tonne blocks that baffle engineering experts today, let alone then. 'For those who have eyes to see, let them see.'

One hundred miles north of Karnak stands the Ptolomic temple of Dendora. In it is staggering star information and astrology. On the west bank of the Nile opposite Luxor is the temple of Deir el Medina. Cartouches and reliefs on its walls depict Ptolomy after death standing in the Grand Hall of Osiris. Ptolomy is having his heart weighed against 'the feather of truth'. Even at that time in history man knew that it was what went on in his heart that would see him through or see him fail.

Ptolomy travelled to the Hall of Osiris after death and this was depicted on the wall of the temple of Deir el Medina, and the Pyramids at Giza mirror Orion's Belt?

The following article appeared in the *Daily Mail* newspaper in England on Friday 13th February 2004.

Oxygen of the stars

The hunt for extraterrestrial life took a leap forward yesterday when scientists revealed they had found oxygen and carbon beyond the solar system. Scientists discovered the two vital elements on the huge planet Osiris, which is 150 light years from Earth.

Astronomers at the Astro-Physics Institute in Paris found the elements using the orbiting 'Hubble' telescope. The findings could lead to the discovery of life on a planet in a distant solar system.

An interesting point to ponder: Christianity's Christ or Christos comes from the Greek Chrestos meaning gentle/kind. Chrestos was one of the epithets traditionally ascribed to Osiris. And significantly, there is an inscription in Delos to Christie Isis.

The priests of the temples of Heliopolis taught of love both divine and physical, that physical love between two people was right and proper and a wonderful gift from spirit. They taught that the female was to be revered,

True spirituality is unaffected by the passage of time. The truth remains the truth forever and needs no amending. That great fountain of truth that was Heliopolis and Alexandria was so important to everyone who has ever lived on this planet during this epoch. The divine knowledge that was given to them was to be imparted to everyone in the world over time via the temples and the huge wondrous structures that were to be a living testament to that truth.

The Pyramids and Sphinx are pointers to the stars of originality (Orion's Belt) and the start of all knowledge. They were built lest we lose our way – and we certainly have, or rather we have been led down the wrong path by our so-called Church faith. The Church teaches you that astrology, tarot and the like are the work of the devil. I tell you now that the devil is the work of the Church.

Now visitors to Egypt look on in awe at the Pyramids and wonder why they were built. The Egyptologists tell us that they are tombs and yet no bodies have ever been found in them. Under the pyramids in chambers yet to be revealed is a library of vast knowledge waiting to be discovered.

Higher evolved beings

High in the mountains of Peru stand the ruins of an ancient city: Machu Picchu. It was built of stone, a stone not found anywhere in the vicinity. It is a stone that had been quarried and hauled many miles then transported up the mountain; another unexplainable engineering feat even by today's standards. Talk to the people of the mountains and they will tell you of silver discs from the sky that land in the lake. These things do not happen regularly but often enough for it not to be the stuff of myth or legend. The local people are not afraid or deterred, neither are they ignorant or crazy. Their minds are not closed by culture, but opened by wisdom. That people there have had meetings with persons who have literally oozed divine love is without question.

Don't be fooled into thinking that spacecraft from another planet or planets are not continually visiting us because they are. They are spotted by civilian aircraft and by US and UK air force jet fighters, but their speed and agility cannot be matched. US air force jets have encountered them on numerous occasions. Pilots filing reports on these incidents learn later that no action is to be taken or that the report has been 'lost'. The pilots and crew are then debriefed that the encounter did not take place. Such reports and sightings will grow as the Earth shift progresses.

So yes, they are here but do not fear them. They are not hostile as in the movie *Independence Day*. They are, don't forget, on a much higher spiritual plane than us. They are here to observe and assist, to enlighten those who seek, not en masse for that would remove our freedom of choice. We must always come to spiritual enlightenment because we want to, not because we are told that it is the thing to do by beings we may well fear.

Higher evolved beings: in essence that is what or who they are. They have been with us for thousands of years, not just since the infamous Roswell incident! They are the one real constant in our history. It is highly likely that it was them who showed the maggi, the spiritually wise ones (the three kings of the stories), the location of Jesus' birthplace. Stars cannot move and relocate over a particular town.

Higher evolved beings are just like the ones that visited those sages all those thousands of years ago. Like the ones spotted by Thutmosis III. That visit was recorded, as many, many others have been for millennia. It seems to this writer that as we battle our way through the second decade in the 21st century sightings are increasing and being reported in the press almost every week. A low craft was spotted and recorded hovering behind a huge cloud at the inauguration of 44th US President Barack Obama in January 2009. Press photographs appeared to confirm its hazy presence. Would our visitors be interested enough to make such a show? Who knows. It is just as easy for them to walk among us – as they surely do. For if a craft was above that inauguration, others surely walked on the ground below.

In talking more of these beings from other worlds it is necessary to remove the cultural dogma that has been propagated and nurtured for many years whether inadvertently or intentionally. With the exception of ET, beings from other worlds, other planets are nearly always portrayed in films and on television as nasty vicious creatures whose only desire is to kill us all and probably destroy the planet as well. In the film 'The Day the Earth Stood Still', as the space ship landed it was surrounded by every kind of military hardware with sufficient firepower to destroy any kind of first contact before anyone even had the chance to set foot on earth's soil with an outstretched friendly hand.

No being other than higher evolved beings would ever be allowed to advance into the realms of inter-stellar travel. Higher evolved beings can, must and do travel to planets, worlds where the inhabitants are spiritual beings on a caporal journey of self discovery. Keeping an eye on them, watching and hoping that they will learn to live together, to look after each other and live a life of peace in harmony with all the creatures sharing the planet with them.

However old you are, you have no doubt been taught that the very mention of 'aliens' and beings from another world, is the stuff of deluded idiots. People from other planets are victims of the same kind of cultural ridicule as ghosts. Just imagine that on your way home tonight, either walking or in your car, you saw a large craft land, people of another world, perhaps even another colour, taller and physiologically different to humans, get out of that craft and walk around. You stare in disbelief and watch them get back into their craft and take off at incredible speed.

Who would you tell? Who could you tell if you did not want to be committed to the nearest secure asylum!

Such is your conditioning and the conditioning of much of the population.

But out there they are. Different body shapes, colours and types for the worlds that they inhabit. The one thing that binds them is that they have evolved. They have evolved past greed, hatred, violence and lies. They are the ones given the ability to traverse the universe watching those who have not yet evolved to such a level.

Native American spiritual leaders have written about vision quests involving 'out of body' experiences in which they have met a myriad of spiritual beings from other worlds. When you do see them there is no fear. The first thing you experience is the overwhelming feeling of love that surrounds them and fills every fibre of their being. You look past the very different shapes, some tall, some short. some with large bulging eyes and some with small 'slits' for eyes. You look past the colours on display – Golden, Blue and yes, green! The shape, colour etc matters not. It is the incredible feeling of love and compassion that fills the very air around them that you instantly become aware of. Their colours, shapes and physiology doesn't matter one jot.

Only when one experiences this do we finally understand what it is like to be universal being. A being who accepts and loves his fellow creatures whether they are red, blue or yellow. It matters not how many eyes a being has or where their ears are! That universal love between everyone and for everyone no matter what body it inhabits is the defining force that should bond us all.

So, please, be like those wonderful few in Peru who accept their visitors as a matter of undisputable fact – and open your eyes in wisdom – not let them be closed by culture. Oh and by the way, those that walk among us are of human form.

Crop Circles: garden rollers and rope??

Firstly lets be clear, the term crop circle is far too simplistic and does not do justice to the phenomenon. Take a look at any website or book showing photographs of 'crop circles' and you will see just how complicated and stunningly beautiful they are. Another point that just about everyone seems to be overlooking is that, like the Nazca lines in Peru, they only take on real form when viewed from the air. Perhaps an overlooked clue to their origin?

When I first started becoming interested in crop circles some years ago I, like many others, was fascinated by the myriad of seemingly complicated patterns on display. We have all seen pictures in the press of crop circles that cover huge areas and the complexity of design is nothing short of breathtaking: patterns that display anything from a depiction of the Mayan calendar to what appears to be a DNA strand.

Like everything else that comes to us from a higher intelligence or indeed from the world of spirit, crop circles have their share of fraudsters, debunkers and 'rational explanations'. The idea that crop circles could be made by a higher intelligence is seen by many as irrational.

Crop circles though, are not a new phenomenon. They have been evident for many hundreds of years and are well documented. Some cryptologists suggest that crop circles are depicted in prehistoric stone and wall carvings, such as in the spiral patterns carved in a stone at Newgrange in Ireland. Crop circles then, are far from new. Just like the higher evolved beings, they have been with us for millennia. So lets take a closer look at them.

It is fast becoming an undisputed fact that crop circles are created as the result of some form of energy interacting with the crops in the field. Men with garden rollers dragging lines of rope and planks into a field is just not a credible theory. Eye-witnesses to crop circles forming (and there have been several) all speak of shafts of light descending from the sky and touching the crop below. This certainly makes sense. For the plants to bend fully to the ground this energy would certainly have to be applied from above.

There are photographs and even a video recording of such incidents. The shafts of light or energy are clearly visible apparently dropping down from cloud level. Within a matter of seconds the 'circle' - however complex, is complete.

So what defines a genuine crop circle, separating it forever from the fraudsters?

In genuine formations the stems of the wheat and barley etc. are not broken but merely bent, normally about an inch off the ground, near the plant's first node. This fact alone defeats the hoax argument, since a plank or garden roller would flatten the crop to the ground, snapping the plants. Scientists believe that the plants have been subjected to a short but incredibly intense burst of heat, enough to soften the plants but not burn them. They fall at 90 degrees where, as they cool, they re-harden undamaged and alive. Plant biologists admit that they are completely baffled by this but it is the surest way to identify a real crop circle from the crude hoax.

It is worthy of note that crop circles largely appear at the intersecting points of the Earth's magnetic pathways of energy.

Here are a few quick facts that should kill off the hoax theories once and for all:

Following the crop circle formation, the laid plants are swirled in mathematical proportions relative to the Golden Mean, the vortex used by nature to create things such as shells.

Genuine crop circles are never round but are slightly elliptical, you cannot achieve that with a roller and a rope.

Often compasses do not work inside a crop circle.

Mobile phones are erratic inside a crop circle.

Animals avoid crop circles.

During a surveillance project in 1989 a Japanese TV crew filmed a crop circle manifesting in the early hours of the morning, showing a swirling motion of energy lasting less than 15 seconds.

At Stonehenge in 1996 an RAF pilot declared nothing to

report when flying over the area of the monument at four-fifteen p.m. but 15 minutes later a second pilot reported a huge 900-foot formation resembling the Julie Set computer fractal. It contained 149 different circles and was aligned along a spiral curve, it lies within view of the very busy monument. It took a team of 11 people five hours to survey the formation.

People have experienced strange and yet wonderful sensations when entering a circle to examine it. There are corroborated reports of one investigator, who was suffering from a dislocated shoulder and was undergoing weeks of physiotherapy, spending all day surveying a circle and when he emerged from it his shoulder was completely healed. He is a scientist, and his doctor confirmed the recovery. It was not an isolated incident.

Let us now deal with the Circle Makers, originally called Team Satan but who changed that name on advice from the media! They hit the headlines in the 1980s saying that they had made the crop circles. They had made a few but they were very crude and basic.

They tried to claim responsibility for the 1996 Stonehenge circle mentioned above, despite the fact that the two RAF pilots as well as a gamekeeper and a security guard all claim that the formation appeared within a 15-minute window.

The media loved the Circle Makers and so did the authorities. Here at last were some folk who could debunk the 'theory' of Extra Terrestrial origin of crop circles. Despite their best efforts working for the BBC and Mitsubishi they only made a crop circle roughly shaped like a van and it took them two whole days.

The evidence, both practical and scientific, in favour of a higher intelligence being the creators of crop circles is overwhelming. Despite this the government and the media continually try to debunk the idea by commissioning TV programmes and newspaper articles to 'expose all crop circles as frauds'. Large swathes of the public agree with the hoax theory, not because they are influenced by such programmes particularly but for a far more base reason.

It is our seemingly in-built inability to conceive a higher intelligence than our own that plunges us into abject denial of anything that requires such thinking – even if the evidence points to the contrary. Man's cultural inability to conceive a higher intelligence than his own will one day be seen as his greatest folly. There are over 200 billion stars in our universe and it is naivety bordering on crass stupidity not to realise that we cannot be alone.

Maybe the higher evolved beings are trying to tell us something very important, without declaring themselves and therefore removing our free will. After all, all they can do is nudge. We should listen.

Perhaps they are saying that the time is now for us not to be consumed with greed and self- importance; that huge corporations and financial institutions should not flourish while countless people starve. Jesus said that at the Earth shift he who is first shall be last. Perhaps we should listen to his words and just maybe we should take notice of our highly evolved visitors, before they really let us know that they are here.

For further reading on Crop Circles I recommend highly: 'Secrets of the Fields' by Freddy Silva.

Human ignorance about planet Earth

Because man sees himself at the 'top of the tree': top of the food chain and endowed with a scientific brain, he sees himself as ruler of the planet and everything on it. He mistakenly believes that he can plunder the planet's resources continually. He has upset the very delicate balance of nature, introducing plant and animal species into areas where they are not indigenous. Chaos has ensued as these introduced species affect the local structure. How far from the teachings of Zep Tepi can we possibly get? Now we find that we 'have to' cull seals because they are affecting fish stocks. (Not that over-fishing to feed an over-populated planet has had any effect, you understand!) To save money on bullets, cubs are clubbed to death. The sad fact is that many, many times they are not actually killed during this process but left bleeding and in excruciating agony. The hard-hearted killers don't care. The angels despair for man – and the seal pup spirits are received home.

In China, puppies and grown dogs are skinned ALIVE for their coats – so that the hair can be used on an array of products for export. The skin, apparently, is easier to remove if the animal is alive. Once the skinning is complete the dogs are thrown in the dirt to die. They too are in excruciating agony as they take their last breaths. Angels receive their spirits home and the perpetrators continue their work in cold, unfeeling ignorance. The dogs are kept in crates close to the skinning area and watch the barbarism in the sure and certain knowledge of the fate that awaits them too.

Foxes are hunted because they kill chickens. Some hunt with traps, some hunt on horseback with hounds that tear the fox to pieces. Man revels in the kill, wiping the blood of the fox on the youngest hunter (mostly children). The men and women drink their wine and talk of a good hunt. The half-starved hounds have done their job. The fox has died a terrible death. Man has revelled in the sight and called it sport. The hunters justify their barbarism now – but they will not be able to later. The angels look on in despair.

According to the Bible, people say, man was given 'stewardship over the animals'. Man has used this over the years as his licence to do with the animals of the Earth exactly what he wants, to treat them exactly as he sees fit, with no emotion or caring for their wellbeing. But to be given stewardship is to be entrusted by spirit to look after the creatures in nature, to care for them and love them. We are all part of the web of life. We are all related.

With the dawning of the new age a new respect for all the creatures of the planet will become a priority. Once hard hearts begin to feel again a new respect will develop – but it will be a slow process, full of reluctance to change.

Our society in the 21st century

I quote now from 'The Last Hours of Ancient Sunlight' by Thom Hartmann

In the 24 hours since this time yesterday thousands of acres of oxygen-making rainforest have been destroyed; the land will be cleared and fenced to raise cattle. Millions of tonnes of toxic chemicals have been released into our environment by industry. Over 45,000 people have died of starvation while many plant and/or animal species have been driven to extinction by the actions of humans.

There are more than 6.5 billion humans on the planet consuming over 50 per cent of the planet's net primary productivity, which is the sum total of food and energy available on the planet.

We consume 62 per cent of the planet's fresh water. Every other life form must fight for the rest.

Every two and a half weeks we add the equivalent of a New York City population to the planet's surface to further suck up the dwindling supplies.

On the average day over 180,000 American school children carry a gun to school.

A recent USA bumper sticker declares, 'Warning: I'm a better Christian clinging to my gun.'

At the turn of the 20th century (1900) 90 per cent of all war casualties were among military personnel. Due to highly efficient weapons that protect soldiers, 90 per cent of the dead in all wars since WW2 have been civilians. And most of the wars that have been fought have been fought over control of resources such as forestland, cropland, oil, coal and minerals.

In January 1999 it was reported that the 7,000-square-mile dead zone in the sea off the Gulf of Mexico had doubled in size since 1992. The area is devoid of fish, shrimp and virtually every other form of life. The cause: 6.5 million metric tonnes of nitrogen dumped as fertiliser on US agricultural land for intensive farms. It makes its way into various waterways, through the Mississippi river and then into the Gulf. Other dead zones are rapidly forming in oceans around the world. Oceanic dead zones do not produce oxygen.

If the governments of the world don't act now, the rainforests will disappear completely in our children's lifetime. No rainforests – NO oxygen.

More than 75 per cent of the topsoil that existed when Europeans first colonised America is now gone.

In contrast to those, like the Native Americans, who live tribally, few people report that they feel even remotely free in our modern society. We are modern day slaves held captive by the slave-holders in our society who use the chains of the mortgage owed to the bank, the loan on the car, the unpaid credit card bills and other cultural everyday, month after month, year after year, links in the cultural slavery chain.

Over the past 42 years the world's population has doubled but there has been a 25-fold increase in violence and brutality.

That is the way of our 'civilised' society, a society of greed and hate.

There are far too many humans on the planet. Far more than the planet can sustain. We use every resource without a thought for those who will follow and have to clear up the mess. We will be knee-deep in waste if we do not act soon.

The planet is overrun with human beings who have little or no consideration or respect for the creatures we share it with. They will be the creators of their own downfall. Man is sawing off the branch he is sitting on. The Earth shift is with us but man will have a hard time before he changes his selfish ways.

Spirituality today

After Jesus, John and Mary's effort to bring us the truth you would have thought that the truth would prevail. You could say that it has in a way. It has prevailed in the Pyramids and the Sphinx on the Giza plateau that still stand today as a testament to Zep Tepi. It has prevailed in the work of the Essenes, the Dead Sea scrolls and the Qumran scrolls. It has prevailed in the continuing work of the Priory of Zion, the original Freemasons and the Knights Templar. It has prevailed despite the best efforts of the Church, who would rather you remained subservient through guilt and fear of hell-fire and eternal damnation.

So now it is up to you to decide where you go from here. I have included a list of titles that you might want to read in order to 'put more meat on the bones' of much of what I have said here. But the real truth that has survived, which I impart to you via this little book, is this: There is no such place as heaven and there is no such place as hell. Such physical places do not exist. We are spiritual beings who have embarked upon a human journey and whilst doing it we inhabit this earthly body. We choose to return to this life in order to grow spiritually and become a more positive spiritual being, so that when we return to spirit we may become closer and more at one with 'God', the great positive energy force that surges through the universe.

Remember that you do not need the Churches to be close to

spirit. Church dogma will make you feel guilty, give you unwanted baggage to carry and restrict your spirit. It will tell you lies.

Swinging incense, prayer mats facing a certain way, praying every half hour, covering certain parts of the body, wearing a particular item of clothing like a cap or a sash, refraining from eating certain foods, fasting (starving yourself!), eating kosher foods – all these are a part of the dogma that smothers and very nearly extinguishes who we really are. They are unnecessary trappings that merely serve to identify which 'faith' you happen to belong to, which man-made institution with its man-made rules you are a part of, which club you are a member of. None, yes NONE of these things are the least bit important to your spirituality.

They are an Earth-bound nonsense.

If any religion that you may follow promotes punishments like floggings and public beatings then they are an abomination to spirit. The cries of the beaten are heard by spirit. Angels despair of the hard hearts of men.

No 'spiritually aware' society can condone such actions. 'Let he among you who has never done anything wrong cast the first stone.'

You carry God or spirit with you in your heart, and it is only by indulging in negative actions that you turn away from the light and harm your spirituality. You are closer to spirit in a garden than you ever will be in a church. Remember that you are a part of 'God', part of the positive spirit, and there are no such things as good and evil as two opposites, just positive and negative karma.

We should try to think, every minute of every day, what we should be doing according to our hearts. We could do no better than to remember what the Native American people had to say on the matter:

Teach your children what we have taught our children, that the Earth is our Mother.

This we know, that the Earth does not belong to man. Man belongs to the Earth.

All things are connected like the blood that unites one family.

Man did not weave the web of life, he is merely a strand in it.

Whatsoever he does to the web, he does to himself.

Treat the Earth and all that dwell thereon with respect, animals, trees, rocks, plants, all things. Help anyone who needs your help, care for anyone who needs your care. Spend a little time each day in seclusion. Talk to your guides and do what you know to be right. Do not put any store by building up riches and wealth in this life. Build up your richness of spirit. Walk the good path and leave tracks for others to follow. Live long and do not fear your death. Never hurt anyone or anything intentionally. When your relatives or friends die they have only returned to spirit. Do not mourn, for you will see them again.

They are whole again and happy.

If you are a materialist and only believe in the here and now, take time out: go sit alone in a forest, away from the hustle and bustle of modern life. Observe nature and let your mind wander to a more spiritual plane. Open up your mind and your heart. It just might change your life.

What have you got to lose?

Angels

People say to me just after they have become more spiritual and have asked the angels for help on some matter, 'What I asked the angels for didn't happen; are you sure that these angels help you?' I must admit that I smile as I say to them that the angels are not here to make things happen for you, or to make your problems go away. They can and sometimes do work with your guide should they need help from a higher level of existence, to point you in the right direction, to give you the strength to see your problems through. Just as your guides do, they inspire you.

Your life problems are yours to face. Your enlightenment comes about because of the way that you deal with the problems that beset you in life. As Orion Mountain Dreamer said in 'The Invitation': 'I want to know if you can face failures and disappointments, yours and mine, and still stand by the lake and shout to the full moon, Yes!' Dealing with your life in a positive way, no matter what befalls you, is enlightening and fulfilling to your spirit on this earthly journey.

So much higher in spirit are the angels, so close to perfection are they, that love and enlightenment through guidance is the gift to us all. I spoke before of the guides we have with us as we make this human journey of further enlightenment. These guides are spirits who are normally on the same level as us in spirit. Occasionally if our situation becomes really difficult in life then our guides may consult an angel or higher level spirit on any matter. We should always be listening to spirit in order for us to live our lives to the full in a spiritual way. We all have a direct line to our guides and the angels, but for most of us the receiver is firmly down.

The point I am trying to get across here is this: You have a direct line to your guides and the angels but you have to *want* to be a deeply spiritual person in every aspect of your life every day. It is all very well calling out to God and anyone who will listen when you are on a 767 airliner travelling through a particularly bad storm. Even the most committed atheist calls then. The astonishing thing is that the person in question could be a real materialist who just lives life for the next buck and considers no one but himself, but he will call upon any God who might be there in an attempt to prolong his life. If such a situation makes that person stop and think about the futility of possessions and wealth then that is good. Sadly, though, for most, once the storm is over, praying is over too until the next time.

It is written: There is no such thing as an atheist on a turbulent aircraft.

Picking up the telephone

The big question I hear you ask is, 'How do I communicate with my spirit guides and the angels?' Well, for most of us it is a one-way street for years. Your guides attempt to influence you in your mind, your thoughts and your decisions as you go through your life. That still small voice in your mind advising you to do what is right is that voice that sometimes you ignore. Loved ones, too, who have passed to spirit; particularly ones who lead spiritual lives may be with us for many years though we do not know it. Vainly they try to influence us to do what is right in love and compassion so that our hearts may be lifted.

The main problem is that over the last 2,000 years spirituality has been replaced by religion. Spirituality remained with the Native Americans, the Aborigines and other indigenous tribes and peoples unaffected by religious influence. These people for the most part had a wonderful connection with nature and therefore with spirit. They knew that they were children of the Earth and that the Earth was their mother. They did not need religion on a Sunday to wash away the materialism and greed of the rest of the week.

We have a long way to go to regain our spirituality but it can be done. It is about changing our mindset. It is about not holding this material world of possessions in high regard at all. It is about reconnecting with nature and through nature reconnecting with spirit in a really big way. And that can be the most difficult thing of all. Do you remember what Jesus said to the rich man who asked what he had to do in order to get into the kingdom of heaven? 'Go and sell all that you have and give it to the poor, then follow me.' It is drastic – too drastic for most people caught in the materialism of the world. And it is a thousand times worse now, with our 'must have' and possession-crazy culture.

What Jesus meant was no more or less than I am saying here. If you are rich or well-off, help people with it by going and visiting countries where the poor are starving, finding out where children are being treated cruelly or where people, animals, forests, anything needs your help and go and give it! Not just by donating sums of money to a charity and considering that your work is done and your conscience appeased, *for it will not be so.*

And never do it grudgingly because you imagine that you are getting a ticket to heaven *because you will not.* What spiritual enlightenment can possibly be gained by writing a cheque, making a donation, setting up a direct debit?

As I have continually stated throughout this book it is what goes on in your heart that counts. It should be and must be seeing the food finally being placed in the starving child's mouth that sends tears cascading down your face. It is seeing the caged animals cared for, seeing the wild habitats preserved or seeing the sick healed that lifts your spirits to the clouds and beyond. Then you will know enlightenment and love. Then your spirit will grow. Then just sit down quietly and say to spirit, 'Now I know. Show me more. Let me do more.'

I said above, *What spiritual enlightenment can possibly be gained by writing a cheque, making a donation, setting up a direct debit?* Of course the answer is none, but that is not to say that we should not respond to appeals on TV for help for any person or animals that need it. But the enlightenment does not come from setting up the direct debit or writing the cheque or quoting a credit card number. Even in this situation the spiritual growth has already taken place. It is what you felt in your heart when you saw the problem, the cruelty, the earthquake or whatever, that brought the tear to your eye and made you decide that you must help. It was the surge of emotion in your heart that brought the tear to your eye and the lump to your throat that made the angels smile.

The next step is to make the world of spirit a larger part of your life. You can do this by seeking like-minded people. You may want to visit a spiritualist church or a clairvoyant, not for a particular reading or a session but just a chat. There are many shops now dealing in spiritual matters; just walk in and say hi! The most important thing you can do is to open up the line of communication from your end. Remember, the world of spirit has been talking to you for years but your telephone receiver has been down. Pick it up!

As I have said before, you can go and sit alone in a garden or wood and just let your mind relax. Forget all the troubles of your everyday life at the moment, for in time they will all pass. Meditate on your existence. Think of you on this planet, here for a reason you do not know. Let your guides fill your mind with light, love and compassion. Let them nudge you and inspire you. Talk to them but remember they know what your needs are before you ask. They will enjoy hearing from you.

You can of course talk to your guides and the angels at any time: walking down the road, driving the car, on a train. Once you have connected with them on that first magical occasion, where you are will not be important. Wherever you are, they will hear you. It is just that if you are establishing communication for the first time it is better for you to do it in a quiet place away from the bustle of modern life and where you can let the real world in.

Finally a word of warning: There are many so-called mind, body and spirit magazines and many, many courses that you can subscribe to, from shamanic to crystal healing, from Tibetan spirituality to drumming. You can spend a lot of money on these magazines and courses. I sometimes fear that the world of mind, body and spirit is becoming as entrenched in dogma as the Church. The only difference is, however, that they are all about spirituality.

I recently spoke to a lady who searched for the truth about life through many courses. She worked with a shaman and did a meditation course to open up the inner child. She did many courses and she took a lot in. She knew her crystals and her rocks. She sat in circles and drummed. She dressed the part and chanted. She meditated and listened to many.

We went out walking and talked a lot about spirit. During our Earthwalks she reconnected with nature and realised that the angels were smiling at her previous in vain attempts to fulfil. She smiled as we talked and she knew that they were listening.

Her heart seemed to open and a realisation came over her. Her connection to spirit is now a fantastic one.

I see many fairs advertised as mind, body and spirit and there are publications also so named. In true spirituality spirit always comes first, then the mind and then the body!

Life's ethical problems

As we journey through this life we encounter many decision-making moments and because we each, individually, see the problem from our own particular viewpoint we all think we know the correct answer to that problem. That's okay if you are dealing with everyday matters like where to eat, when to eat, which movie is good and which one is not. No one but you is going to be adversely affected by your decisions. When it comes to ethical questions, however, it is just not that simple. Ethics are all about being morally correct and honourable. Any decisions made affect the lives of others. Differing opinions cause moral dilemmas.

And therein lies the problem. What is right and morally correct for one person is not so for another. Different viewpoints are formed from different life experiences and influences, so it stands to reason that there will be a myriad of differing opinions. Where spirituality is lost, nurture is all that remains. And it is your nurture that forms your opinions.

With a real knowledge of spirituality, however, all ethical questions can be answered. The answers will not please anyone still viewing the question from a nurture or cultural viewpoint.

Abortion and euthanasia are perhaps the two biggest issues causing moral dilemmas. I will now examine these two very important issues from a spiritual viewpoint.

Abortion

At the very extreme side of the argument against abortion are the so-called 'Pro-lifers'. These people argue that the right of the unborn child to be born is paramount, even in the case of someone who has been raped. The Pro-lifers appear to be supported in their opinions by the Church of Rome, the Catholic Church, who assert that 'all life is sacred'.

This is an entrenched viewpoint that has no room for compassion. For whatever situation you ask them about (and there are plenty of websites where you can check this out) the stock answer is always in favour of the unborn child. Nothing else matters. Health issues, condition of the unborn foetus, health of the pregnant woman or circumstances of conception – all are discarded in favour of the blanket argument: no to abortion. The argument is black and white. There are no grey areas in their point of view, no individual circumstances to be considered, no human emotions, no compassion. But, dear friends, life is not black and white. It was never designed to be that simple. Life is a million shades of grey! That is the very reason we are here. If every decision was black and white with no compassion involved then the human race would surely implode upon itself.

The argument of the right of the unborn child leads me to state that once again the advice of the Catholic Church is incorrect.

Terminating a foetus at 21 weeks is not murder, for it is a fact that the spirit does not usually enter the body of the foetus until birth or even some few days later in extreme cases. The exceptions are those who wish to go through the birth experience for some reason.

When a woman considers abortion, she does so with a heavy heart. She wrestles with both scenarios in her mind. She should ask her guides what she should do. Do not run away with the idea that they will advise her always to go through with the pregnancy, for they do not. Much depends upon the reasons she chose this particular human journey; what lessons she wished to learn in this life; the things she needed to experience in order for her spirit to progress and grow. Sometimes, despite guides trying to advise, the wrong decision is made. And that wrong decision can just as easily be to go through with the pregnancy as it can be to terminate it.

Most people are not even aware of their guides. Whatever the scenario or the outcome, there is no judgement from them, just more help as the life path changes.

Those women who have been raped, whatever their age, should abort that foetus if they are so traumatised by the terrible act of rape that they feel they cannot go through with the pregnancy. There is no judgement to be made by anyone. No one can make that decision but the person concerned, with the influence of her guides. Pro-lifers cannot put themselves in the position of any female who does not want to go through with her pregnancy. They have not lived her life, had her experiences or endured her hardships. The only person who can decide whether or not to have the baby is the pregnant female; it is her life, her experiences, and her decision. There is not, nor will there ever be, any kind of judgement for her by the spirit world. Nor should there be any kind of judgement by those on Earth who think they know better.

The Church's idea of the sanctity of life for the unborn is incorrect. The Church has caused enough misery for women with their ridiculous anti-contraception stance. That idea has seen a veritable explosion in unplanned and sometimes unwanted pregnancies, causing heartache and misery for families already struggling under such idiotic dogma.

Euthanasia

'We put down a really sick dog,' I often hear people say, 'but we let human beings suffer!' This statement is largely true; of course the human race does do just that. We seem to have unlimited compassion for our pets but seem to want to hang on to human life long after any quality of life for the person involved has evaporated.

Enter the argument Pope Benedict, God bless him, who stated in 2009 with typical religious indifference that perhaps the suffering is all part of God's wonderful plan for us and that we should endure it – or words to that effect.

Well, God doesn't have a wonderful plan for us – we do! We plan with our guides and the angels themselves each life journey that will enable us to experience decisions and actions that will touch the lives of others and let our spirits grow. The gradual – and most times too gradual – ceasing up of the human body and/or mind is not part of any experience that we should want to endure or subject our relatives and friends to.

Suicide, as I said earlier, is about the only thing that upsets the spirit world. It is a waste of a body. Suicide in the young is particularly frowned upon in spirit. No judgement still, no telling off, no lake of fire – just love and light. But it is still, say the spirits, a waste!

But there is no waste in the termination of a life that sees the body deteriorating to the point of being unable to function – or the mind deteriorating into oblivion. Those people who elect to go abroad to end their lives do so because they know that what lies ahead is a slow, lingering and perhaps painful death.

If a person is terminally ill, relying on constant care, losing control of limb movements or the capacity to think and/or remember, these things remove any quality of life and quickly make the living of life intolerable for them. And that is the key. It should and must always be the decision of the person who is losing their quality of life and no one else's. Euthanasia is a merciful release for them. So long as we remember that no family member or lawyer should be able to make that decision for a person just because they have 'become a burden' or because the children want to sell the house!

Once someone has made the decision to end the pain and suffering by ending their life, then family and friends should offer 100 per cent support and love.

I have heard it said that occasionally some family members feel that the person concerned is being selfish, denying the family of future days, weeks and perhaps months in their company. I am sure that the person who has chosen euthanasia has not done so to spite the family in any way. They have invariably despaired and cried uncontrollably as their quality of life slips away and they are no longer able to do the simplest things. An active and alert mind watches helplessly as family and friends care for a once useful body. I cannot imagine what it must be like to gradually lose control of my limbs, bodily functions or mind. I should think that I too would want to slip quietly away.

Euthanasia can be a happy release – no matter how sad those who are left behind may be. Their sadness demonstrates their love. What relatives must remember is that it is not all about them. It is all about ending the suffering of a loved one with compassion, dignity and heartfelt love. The angels welcome the spirit home. No judgement. No lake of fire. Just love.

The fifth world of peace

The above are just two ethical questions that can, in today's society, cause disagreement and debate; all so very unnecessary when viewed from the point of view of spirituality.

If you remove the influence of religion, which is intransigent, unyielding and hardline, buried deep in its own overbearing dogma, then you will be well on the way to finding the correct answer. Then you have to view the world in which we live from the point of view that all of us are spiritual beings on a human journey who should be living a life with respect and love for all people, the animals and the planet itself, all the time aware that we are not alone and that the spiritual world is all around us. Add to that a knowledge of the ways of spirit then think with your heart in overdrive and overwhelmed by compassion for the person concerned and you should come to the correct conclusion. Here's hoping!

In closing, I await the day when the peoples of this planet will become true spiritual beings with full knowledge of harmony and compassion. When the veil of materialism, greed, separatism and prejudice is lifted from the minds of everyone, and men (and women) can peacefully co-exist for the benefit not of the self but for the other.

I await a time when the thought is not – 'what can I get' but 'what can I give'. A time when we can look at those less fortunate without ridicule or derision and lend a helping hand up.

This wonderful world chockfull of spirituality and peace will be a world where the power of our minds can be used to heal and start anew; where that power can be used in unity with the angels, when needed, to accomplish things that at the moment man is not able to do – because of his spiritual blindness. The power of positive thought is without end.

When greed and possessions fall away, the fifth world of peace will truly be upon us. Then our possibilities will be endless.

Chronology

Following is a complete chronology of what has happened since the time of Zep Tepi, some of which is not featured in this book anywhere else. These events add weight to our findings.

Time	Event
10,500BC	The first visit during the old age to enlighten the inhabitants of this planet at Egypt. Heliopolis is born. The Sphinx and Pyramids are constructed as per sky/ground correlations. The 4th Epoch of this planet begins. The Mayan Temples at Angkor Watt are constructed as per sky/ground correlations.
10,000BC	*The Encyclopaedia of Dates and Events* by E.L. Pascoe sets this time as a possible date of the first occupation of America by man. He appears to have crossed the Bering Straits from Asia.
9,000BC	Wooden 'totem pole' circle built at Stonehenge in Wiltshire, England.
4,700BC	Carnac, northern France: an earthen mound with a megalithic passageway oriented to the winter solstice is constructed.
4,000BC	Megalithic temples are constructed on Malta.
3,500BC	Qumran relics date from this time. At this time the settlement was a Bedouin camp.

3,000BC	Henges are built at Thornborough in Yorkshire, England to mirror Orion's Belt and are aligned to the sunrise at the solstices. On Callanish on the Outer Hebrides a stone circle is built to draw attention to an obscure lunar phenomenon known as 'The southern extreme of the moon's lunar standstill', which happens every 19 years. Callanish is aligned to sunrise and sunset on the spring and autumn equinoxes.
2,600BC	Stonehenge is built by the Druids on the site of the earlier totem pole circle. Stonehenge aligns through the heelstone to the summer solstice sunrise and the winter solstice sunset.
1,970BC	Sesostris III erects an obelisk at Heliopolis, Egypt. It remains today at the site, now part of northern Cairo.
1,500BC	The island of Thera, north of Crete is totally destroyed by a volcano. This forms the basis for Plato's 'Atlantis' story.
1,440BC	Moses leaves Mount Herob in Sinai and journeys back to the priests of Heliopolis in order to show his people 'The Way'. The return journey takes 40 days and 40 nights. The Bible tells us he has 'tablets of stone' carrying the ten commandments.
1,372BC	Amenhotep IV, later Akhenaten (pleasing to Aten), replaces the religion of Amun with the profoundly mystical and monotheistic religion of Aten, in which all men are equal in the love of an only god, based on knowledge he gained from Heliopolis. He marries beautiful Nefertiti, a Mitannian princess. Abraham spends four years with Akhenaten and takes on board the 'religion' of the Heliopolan priests.

955BC	King Solomon builds a temple on Mount Moriah specifically to house the Ark of the Covenant, itself home to the precious 'tablets of stone'.
660BC	A Jewish temple is built on Elphantine island near Aswan, Egypt (close to Philae island and the Temple of Isis) to house the Ark of the Covenant after Jerusalem's ruler turns pagan.
587BC	Jerusalem falls to the Babylonians. Solomon's Temple is destroyed.
570-500BC	Greek philosopher Pythagoras predicts a new world order at what will turn out to be year zero. Thus the BC countdown was used long before the birth of Jesus. He was actually seven years adrift when applied to Jesus but absolutely spot on when applied to Jesus' brother James.
470BC	The Jewish temple on Elphantine island is under threat by invading Persians. The Ark is carried again to Ethiopia via Sudan. It is a journey that takes many years, the Ark finding brief homes along the way.
400BC	The Nag Hammadi texts are buried in Egypt. These venerate the role of the female and of sexuality.
130BC	King Antioches of Syria foists a new system of Greek worship upon the Jewish community. They walked out en masse to form their own pure community in the wilderness at Qumran, with mainly Essene and Gnostic ways.
31BC	Jewish historians describe a violent earthquake in Judea. At this time there is a break in the two known settlements at Qumran. The second settlement began during the reign of Herod the Great (37–4BC).
26BC	Jesus' mother Mary is born (she has Jesus when she is 19).

7BC	Jesus is born on 9th March.
5BC	Herod's decree means that Joseph, Mary and Jesus flee to Egypt.
0BC	Jesus' brother James is born.
AD12	Jesus spends a number of years with the Essenes at Qumran. He then travels back to Egypt and meets Mary Magdalene. She is a high priestess at the Temple of Isis on the island of Philae. Jesus becomes an initiate.
AD30	September: Mary Magdalene anoints Jesus' feet at their first marriage.
AD32	December: Mary conceives.
AD33	March: Jesus is crucified but survives. Following the crucifixion Joseph of Arimathea, (James, Jesus' brother) is imprisoned for a short time. Then Mary, Joseph, Martha and Lazarus go to France. Mary gives birth to a daughter, Tamar.
AD35	Joseph/James arrives at Marseilles. He then crosses to Britain, arriving in the west country where he is greeted by King Arviragas of Siluria, brother of Charactacus the Pendragon, and granted 12 hides of land at Glastonbury.
AD36	Jesus rejoins Mary. She conceives again in December.
AD37	Mary gives birth to a son, Jesus Justus.
AD40	Jesus is in Damascus and confronts Saul. He is 'converted' and starts to preach the resurrection.
AD40s	Peter and Paul are in Antioch. James and the Nazarenes are in Jerusalem. Simon Zealotes is with the Gnostics in Cyprus.

AD44	The political situation worsens and Mary returns again to Gaul. With her are Martha, Lazarus, Marcella, Phillip the apostle, Mary Jacob and Mary Salome (Helena). Later that year Mary gives birth to a second son, called Joseph. Today the town is known as Les Saintes Maries de la Mere. Jesus is reported to have gone to Galatia in Asia Minor. Could he have in fact have gone to Ethiopia, itself known as part of the Indias?
AD46	Jesus Justus is nine years old and being schooled in Caesarea.
AD49	Jesus Justus goes to Britain with his uncle James/Joseph.
AD53	Jesus Justus is officially proclaimed crown prince at the synagogue in Corinth and receives the Davidic crown prince's title of Justus, succeeding his uncle James/Joseph.
AD60	Jesus the Christ goes to Rome via Crete and Malta. During his stay, Jesus Justus is also in the city. Paul returns to Jerusalem having travelled extensively with Luke. At the same time Jesus' other son Joseph has finished his education at the Druidic College and has settled in Gaul with his mother.
AD62	James/Joseph is spiritually excommunicated in Jerusalem.
AD63	Mary Magdalene dies aged 60 at St Baume in Southern France. She is buried at St Maximus in Provence.
AD65	Christians are relentlessly persecuted by Nero. They are tortured and burnt. He engulfs Rome in flames and blames the Christians. He has both Peter and Paul put to death. Remaining Nazarenes leave Jerusalem for Jordan led by Simon Zealotes.

AD66	Fighting between Romans and Zealots in Caesarea. Hostility quickly engulfs the city. Zealots hold the city for four years. Roman governors order all public records in Jerusalem destroyed in order to prevent any future access to Jesus' family genealogy.
AD70	Massive Roman army led by Flavius Titus lays Jerusalem to waste. The Temple falls. Inhabitants are slaughtered and survivors sold as slaves. The Holy City is an empty ruin for the next six decades. Qumran also falls. Mark's gospel is composed without the resurrection. That is a later spurious addition.
AD74	September: Jesus Justus marries the granddaughter of Niccodemus. Mountain fortress of Masada, southwest of the Dead Sea, falls. A thousand Jews had withstood repeated sieges by Roman soldiers; gradually deprived of all supplies they opted for mass suicide. Only two women and five children survive. One historian claims that Jesus Christ died at Masada during the long siege.
AD80	Gospel of Luke, a Greek doctor, is composed for a high ranking Roman official.
AD82	James/Joseph of Arimathea dies at Glastonbury on 27th July.
AD85	Gospel of Matthew is composed. More than half of it is derived directly from Mark's.
AD100	John's gospel is composed in Greece. The author is unknown. This gospel differs from the other three. There is no nativity scene; in fact no description of Jesus' birth. It contains events not found in the other gospels: the wedding at Cana, the roles of Nicodemus and Joseph of Arimathea and the raising of Lazarus (although the latter was once in Mark's gospel!).

AD314	Roman Emperor Constantine the Great changes Jesus' official birthday from March to 25th December. The reason was twofold: it separated it from any Jewish occasion and it would coincide with and replace the pagan sun festival (solstice).
AD367	Athanasius of Alexandria compiles a list of the works to be included in the New Testament.
AD391	Christians burn the Serapium Library at Alexandria.
AD393	The list of works to be included is ratified by the Church Council of Hippo.
AD397	The list of works is then ratified by the Council of Carthage. of some fifty-eight works, five are chosen. They are altered and their content amended to reflect Church policy. New phrases are added to Jesus' ministry.
AD700	The Saxons rebuild the Glastonbury Church complex.
AD1059	Renne le Château in southern France is consecrated to Mary Magdalene.
AD1099	Jerusalem is occupied by Christian armies (until the recapture by Saladin in 1187). The Priory of Sion is founded, otherwise known as the Order of Sion or the Order of Our Lady of Zion. The reported aim of the society was to protect the descendants of the Merovingian dynasty in southern France. They were devoted to Mary Magdalene, later forming the Templars.

AD1112	St Bernard of Clairvaux teaches Cistercian monks sacred geometry and the nature of the Grail writings. This was later corrupted by them into the Grail stories heard today. Bernard writes of Mary Magdalene, comparing her to the Ark. St Bernard works on the Templars Cathedral at Chartres, France.
AD1119	Hugh de Payens and Godfrey de St Omer form the Knights Templar, known at that time as the guardians of Solomon's Temple. One of the original nine knights is an uncle of St Bernard of Clairvaux. They travel to Jerusalem and King Baudouin installs them at the site of Solomon's Temple itself. The Templars excavate extensively under the site.
AD1126	Hugh de Payens suddenly leaves Jerusalem for Europe with Andre de Montbard, uncle of St Bernard.
AD1127	Most of the original nine Knights return to Europe to a hero's welcome, mostly orchestrated by St Bernard.
AD1134	St Bernard influences the building of the north tower of Chartres Cathedral in France and the installation of statues depicting the Ark of the Covenant leaving for Ethiopia and many of Mary Magdalene. This section of the Cathedral is known as 'The Doorway of the Initiates'.
AD1139	Pope Innocent II issues a papal bull proclaiming that the Knights Templar serve no authority other than the Vatican.
AD1182	Cistercian monks compose the first recorded Grail story.
AD1184	Disastrous fire at Glastonbury after which Henry II grants a 'Charter of Renovation' in which Glastonbury is referred to as 'The mother and burying place of the saints founded by the disciples of our Lord themselves'.

AD1185	A stone 'Lady Chapel' is added to the Glastonbury complex. A group of Templars go to Ethiopia in search of the Ark of the Covenant.
AD1188	Wolfram von Eschenbach startswork on *Parzival*, the Grail story featuring characters who parallel those of Solomon, Sheba and their son Melenic. These stories are based on information discovered during the European occupation. Wolfram's *Parzival* mentions the precession of the planets and its effect upon us all. Astrology! The Priory of Zion and the Knights Templar become two separate organisations.
AD1207	Pope Innocent III unleashes the Albegensian Crusade. What followed was one of the greatest massacres in history in the name of religion. The entire population of the Languedoc in southern France was murdered. The area was the home of Mary Magdalene, her family and the bloodline of Mary and Jesus Christ. The final town to fall was Beziers. It fell with total annihilation of its people on 12th July, the feast day of Mary Magdalene. It took 40 years to achieve this goal and the entire area known as the Languedoc was plunged from an advanced society into a barbarous, dark time. The Cathars, along with all of Mary and Jesus' descendants, were murdered.
AD1250	The Cistercean monks turn the Grail into a cup that caught the blood of Christ. Dominican Archbishop of Genoa Jacobus de Voragine writes *The Golden Legend* in which he refers to Mary Magdalene as both Illuminator and Illuminated; these are roles claimed for her by the forbidden Gnostic texts.

AD1307	13th October: On secret orders from the French King Phillip the Fair and with the backing of a papal bull, the Knights Templar are arrested, tortured and burnt. Many Knights flee to Scotland, whose king does not recognise papal orders. The secret Priory of Zion lives on.
AD1308	Templar ships arrive at what is now known as Cape Cod, America (Merica).
AD1398	Master Alchemist Nicolas Flamel becomes grand master of the Priory of Zion.
AD1500	Leonardo da Vinci paints 'The Last Supper' and 'Adoration of the Magi'. In both paintings he depicts himself as looking away from the holy scene. Da Vinci was a member of the Priory, spending his last nine years as its grand master.
AD1535	Muslim hoards attack Axum in Ethiopia and raze to the ground the ancient and most holy Church of Saint Mary of Zion. During their 15-year occupation much of the Christian manuscripts, icons and paintings as well as the churches were destroyed and treasures were looted. The Ark was safe, having been taken temporarily back to an island monastery on Lake Tana, Daga Stephanos.
AD1578	Michel de Nostredame is elected grand master of the Priory of Zion.
AD1595	Robert Fludd, a Rosicrucian, is elected grand master of the Priory of Zion.

AD1650	James Burke of Kinnaird, a Scottish Freemason and much learned of ancient languages and treasures, journeys to Ethiopia. He copies by hand the Book of Enoch. This book is the oldest Jewish mystical literature of great significance to Freemasons. Certain rituals within Enoch liken him to the Egyptian god of wisdom, Thoth. According to the book Enoch was a great inventor of writing and taught men the art of building and of the 'great secret'. This great secret is engraved on a white perphyl stone in the bowels of the Earth.
AD1770	Burke arrives in Ethiopia on 17th January to view the 'Tinket', a celebration during which the Ark of the Covenant makes one of its rare public appearances. He does not gain access.
AD1885	The tiny French village of Renne le Château receives a new parish priest. A few miles to the southeast are the ruins of a medieval fortress, once a home of the Knights Templar. A mile east of Renne stands the ruins of the Château de Blanchefort, ancestral home of Bernard de Blanchefort, fourth grand master of the Knights Templar.
AD1896	After discovering some parchments whilst renovating his small church, the priest Sauniere becomes fabulously wealthy and begins an extensive programme of building as well as excavating and investigating the surrounding area. His great knowledge of 'the secret' leads him to build a new chapel at Renne that is full of cryptic clues to his discovery: a Scottish child in a kilt, a depiction of Jesus being carried away from the tomb at night, echoes of Solomon's Temple and many references to Mary Magdalene, the Knights Templar and the Priory of Zion. Already friendly with his young housekeeper at the outset of his discovery, he now no longer fears death or the dogma of the Church and openly takes her as his lover.

AD1917	January 17th: Sauniere dies. Having called a priest from a nearby district and told him of his knowledge, the visiting priest refused to offer Extreme Unction to the dying man and left the property ashen and visibly shaken. In her final days, Sauniere's young mistress promised to tell a close friend about the secret knowledge but suffered a massive stroke that rendered her unable to speak. When she died the secret 'died' with her.

Further reading and bibliography

I end with a list of further reading. Reading the books in this list will help you to put more meat on the bones of what I have written here. For I have no physical proof that what I say is correct save the events and texts carried throughout history – and a wonderful knowledge that has arrived (by the bucket load) with a state of knowing.

The Holy Blood and theHoly Grail	Michael Baigent, Richard Leigh and Henry Lincoln
The Templar Revelation	Lynn Picknett and Clive Prince
Mary Magdalene, Christianity's Hidden Goddess	Lynn Picknett
Heaven's Mirror	Graham Hancock and Samantha Faiia
Between Death and Life	Dolores Cannon
Bury My Heart at Wounded Knee	Dee Brown
Bloodline of the Holy Grail	Laurence Gardner
The Last Hours of Ancient Sunlight	Thom Hartmann
The Last Pope	John Hogue

The Hiram Key	Robert Lomas and Christopher Knight
Keeper of Genesis	Robert Bauval and Graham Hancock
Sacred Path Cards	Jamie Sams
Secrets of the Fields	Freddy Silva

For further information please visit www.nealsutton.co.uk